I Want Her

Shannon Bliss

Copyright © 2024 by SHANNON BLISS

All rights reserved.

No portion of this book may be reproduced in any form without written permission from the publisher or author, except as permitted by U.S. copyright law.

Contents

(1) Goodbye High school!   1

(2) Bae Watch   5

(3) Lights, Camera, Hottie   10

(4) Jerk Face   16

(5) The Plan   23

(6) Knock Knock   34

(7) We Meet Again   42

(8) Getting Somewhere   49

(9) And You Are?   61

(10) At Night   67

(11) Your Fault   75

(12) Shopping   82

(13) Friends?   89

(14) Weird Things   98

(15) Thank You   104

(16) And Who's This? 114
(17) Gala Shopping 124
(18) The Gala 135
(19) Cruise 147
(20) A Drunken Ashley 153
(21) What Happened? 163
(22) The Beach 174
(23) Emotions 181
(24) We're back 190
(25) The Doctor's Visit 198
(26) Problems 207
(27) Where Am I? 212
(28) The Mole 219
(29) Torture 229
(30) Mission: Ashley 234
(31) I'm Better 240
(32) Friendly Intruders 248
(33) SUPRISE?! 255
(34) A New Plan 266
(35) Here it Goes 275

(1) Goodbye High school!

Ashley's POV

I woke up this morning glad that high school was finally over. No more annoying teachers, or horny jocks, or even the weird nerds. But I also felt sad. I mean don't get me wrong, high school was a complete bore, but I'm gonna miss all the people that I cared about. Like the teacher who gave me food or my friends that were in different grades and even my friends that were graduating.

"Ashley Rowens." Once I heard my name I snapped out of it. The fear and the joy going through me as I thought about the people I was sort of leaving behind disappeared and all I could think about was graduating. As I walked onto the stage with peers in front of me and behind me, I smiled. I heard my family shouting and cheering my name. I shook my teachers' hands as they congratulated me. I walked off the stage and sat in my seat. As soon as I sat down, I received a text from Taylor, my best friend.

Best friend- Girl we finally made it through this hell hole.

Me- I know right. Now we're off to have one of the best years together until college next fall.

Best friend- You don't have to tell me twice. We're definitely going to some concerts.

Me- Hell yeah we are.

When I looked up, I noticed everyone was starting to stand and I was so confused. The guy next to me tapped me on the shoulder and pointed to our caps. I smiled and he chuckled.

"Three, two, one!" Everyone counted down and we threw our caps high into the air and smiled. It was hard for me to catch mine, but I did. We flipped our tassels and I gave the people near me a hug to congratulate them. Everyone parted ways to go see their families or just left.

I am a pretty short person at around 5 feet 3 inches so it was hard for me to find my family. They kept texting me and my phone was just going crazy. When I found my family, they all had smiles on their faces. My younger brother, Ethan, had headphones on, but still gave me a hug to congratulate me.

"So what does it feel like to be a free young lady?" My dad asked.

"Well it feels pretty good....now that I don't have to wake up early in the morning to go to school." My dad and mom laughed at my reply.

"ASHLEEEYY!" I knew that voice way to well. I spun around quickly to see Taylor running at me with the biggest smile plastered on her face.

I ran towards her and we gave each other a hug as we bumped into each other.

"We did it, we did it, we did it!" She did a happy dance and kept singing those words. Her parents walked over to mine and greeted each other.

"Taylor, you sound like Dora when you say that." I looked at her as if she were crazy.

She stopped dancing and looked at me with a dead panned face. "You just had to take the joy didn't you Swiper? Swiper no swiping, Swiper no swiping." We both started laughing.

Her parents and my parents congratulated both of us. "Ashley, we have a surprise for you waiting at home." My parents said with a smile.

I was wondering what it could be. Could it be plane tickets or concert tickets or a car? Until Taylor gasped.

"Mom, dad can I go with Ashley to see what it is pleeeassee?" She had her hands in front of her face with her fingers interlocked. Her parents and my parents exchanged looks and her parents nodded.

"Thank you soooo much." She gave her parents and big hug and kissed both of their cheeks. Then she ran and grabbed my hand. "Okay Rowens, what are we waiting for?" She was too excited to find out what MY surprise was.

We all got into my dad's SUV and drove to my house. When we pulled into the driveway, my dad opened the garage and I almost died.

"YOU GUYS GOT ME A CAR?!?!" I was so excited to have my first car. I jumped out of my dad's car and so did Taylor. We started squealing like freaking pigs. When my dad and mom stepped out of the car, they said surprise. And I had tears welling up in my eyes. I gave them a very tight hug and said thank you. They handed me the keys and I was sooooo, freaking happy. It was the car that I've been dreaming of since freshman year. It was a matte black Jeep Wrangler, hard top convertible.

I unlocked my new car and got in it. I took my drivers test and passed on the first try. I even had my license, I just didn't have a car to use it with until now. I was unbelievably excited. My brother walked to my car and turned to my parents with a shocked expression.

"When am I getting my first car? I want an all black Ford F-1" My dad and my mom laughed.

"Hold on Tiger. You gotta be old enough to drive first." My dad grabbed onto my brother's shoulder and my brother looked heartbroken. Everyone except for my brother started laughing.

This day couldn't get any better. I finally left high school, I got a car, it was summer and the weather was wonderful. How could this day get any better?

"Oh honey, we're also having a cookout. Your grandparents, aunts, uncles and cousins are coming. So are a few of my friends." My dad said before he would forget.

I was even more excited, because if family was coming over that meant I was going to get gifts and money. And I could show off my new car. My house is pretty big in case you're wondering. It has 4 bedrooms, a guest room and 6 and a half bathrooms. We also have a workout room and movie room in our basement. Our house has 4 levels and that includes the basement. Our backyard is even cooler, we have a patio and a fire pit in our backyard. We also have a nice size pool that goes to 15 feet, and has a diving board.

(2) Bae Watch

Ashley's POV

"I need a boyfriend." I said with a pout. I can't believe I've never had a boyfriend, yet I could. All the boys at my school are fuckboys. They're always trying to get in your pants or want a blow job, and I wasn't ready to do that yet. Boys are..... horn dogs. Yep, that's what they are. They're walking dicks.

"You and I both." Taylor said as if she was stating a fact. She was sitting on my bed on her phone. She kept smiling and giggling and I thought something was wrong with her. I've never seen her so focused. Usually she'll text someone then turn off her phone. But not this time, this time she held on to it, like she was excited to talk to this person.

"Who is it?" I asked and Taylor looked up at me with a confused face.

"What?" Taylor smiled tightly and blushed. "It's no one."

I got up from my desk and belly flopped onto my bed, right next to her. "It's obviously not 'no one' because someone has you smiling like the joker." I chuckled

She tilted her head down and her eyes moved up to look at me. Then she smiled a huge smile and asked. "Why so serious?" We both started to laugh. If you don't get it, then oh well.

"C'mon Tay. I'm your bestest friend in the whole frickin' world so just tell me." I whined. I furrowed my eyebrows and stuck out my bottom lip.

"Fiiine. It's this guy, that went to our school. His name is Joseph. He's soo fucking hot!" She was blushing hard and smiling and obviously day dreaming about this guy.

"Show me a picture." I demanded excitedly.

She went to his Instagram page and let me scroll through his pictures. He was hot. He was Hispanic and an athlete. He played LAX (lacrosse) and soccer but this guy was ripped. How haven't I not noticed him before. Like I've never seen him.

"Don't like any of the pictures though. I don't want him to think I'm stalking him." She jumped and her eyes were wide. I laughed.

"Oops." Is all I said and she looked scared and furious.

"You did not. Oh my God. Ashley fucking Rowens. Did you just.... Give me my phone right now." I jumped off my bed and ran out my room. She was running after me with a scrunched up face. I couldn't help but laugh. I ran out the house and into the front yard and I tripped. But I didn't cry, cause I am a big girl and big girls don't cry. Instead I just started laughing hard. My eyes were watery and my stomach hurt but I couldn't help it.

"Which one did you like? Hurry up Ashley, I don't want him to notice." I sat up, recovering from the fit of laughter and shook my head. "What do you mean no?" Taylor looked taken back.

"I didn't like any of his pictures." I said smiling. She rubbed her eyes and stood up.

"I know you didn't just tell me that you liked a picture, then ran away with my phone, when I almost tripped going down the stairs, just to tell me you never liked any of the pictures." She bit her bottom lip, she wasn't too mad, but she wasn't very happy. "You're gonna get it."

" Well to be fair, I never said that I liked a picture. All I said was 'oops' and you assumed that I liked a picture. And you didn't have to chase me." I stood up and dusted my knees and butt off. She looked mad but then she started laughing as if she was insane.

"It's on like Donkey Kong. I'm gonna get you back." Taylor and I love joking around with each other, but this time, I feel as if I'm going to regret messing with her.

We walked to the kitchen and Taylor sat on the counter. I don't know why she chooses not to sit on the stools we have for the counter. I went to the fridge and got a bottle of water.

"Can you get me a bottle too?" Taylor asked. She was on that stupid phone of hers, talking to some stupid guy.

"Yup." I tossed the bottle at her lightly and she freaked out. She almost threw her phone so that she could catch the water bottle, but she didn't.

"Hey." She furrowed her eyebrows. "What was that for? I could've broken my phone."

I smiled. "Oops?" I shrugged my shoulders and giggled.

She scooted off the counter so she could get her water that was laying on the ground.

"How about this? We can go to the movies together and go look for a bae?" Taylor said as she hopped back onto the counter. It sounds like a good idea, the only thing I'm worried about is having to approach the guy. I have no problems with a guy coming up to me, but I'm nervous about making the first move.

"Sounds good. But we need to invite some more people, cause I need someone who's not currently crushing on someone to help me find a bae." Taylor smiled and nodded.

"True. I'll text Ayanna and Claudia, and tell them we are going on bae watch." Taylor looked at me for confirmation and I nodded my head. She instantly started texting them.

"Wait, but what movie are we going to go see?" I asked. Because going to the movies and not having a plan isn't the best since everyone will argue about it there and we might split up to see different movies.

"Oh yeah. We could go see Suicide Squad." She looked up at me.

"Oh my God, I really want to see that. When does it come out. We have to go the day it comes out because that's when everyone goes to see that movie. Even boys." I smiled when I said boys. Thinking of all the possibilities that could happen, like meeting a hot, nice guy that isn't worried about getting into your pants.

"Alright I'll just ask them and then we got ourselves our bae watch date." Taylor started typing into her phone and soon you would hear her text tone go off, signifying a new text. "Okay Ayanna and Claudia are both in. Looks like we are on bae watch."

"Okay seriously, stop saying that."

"Stop saying what?"

"Bae watch. It's really annoying and just.... I don't know. It's weird." Taylor looked at me with a dead panned expression.

"Too bad I like that word. Bae watch, bae watch, bae watch, bae watch."

I groaned and walked upstairs to my room, with Taylor laughing in pursuit.

(3) Lights, Camera, Hottie

Ashley's POV

"Get in bitches." Taylor yelled at Ayanna and Claudia from inside my car. I had to pick up Ayanna and Claudia, since they live near each other, Ayanna walked over to Claudia's house.

"Ash, your car is nice!" Ayanna commented. The top was off, and she could see the inside of my car from outside of it. She got in and started feeling the seats and was looking in all the nooks and crannies. Ayanna had a big smile on her face.

"Your car is really nice." Claudia said. She got in and buckled up. "I wish my parents would buy me a car, but they said I have to get a used one before I get a new one." She pouted.

"Are you guys buckled up because I'm not trying to get a ticket?" They nodded and we were off.

I blasted some music so we could hear it over the wind. I loved the feeling of the wind through my hair and on my face. We were all singing Child's Play by Drake and it was just the best thing.

When we got to the movies it was 8:00 pm and the movie starts at 8:40, so we decided to walk around the plaza. The movie theatre was in the middle of a shopping plaza, with restaurants, clothing stores, grocery stores and a sport store. We were walking from store to store and just having so much fun that we barely realized that we had 8 minutes to get back to the theatre and get our seats. The good thing about our movie theatre is that you can purchase tickets online and you're seat is reserved.

I heard a bunch of guys laughing and my head snapped to see where it was coming from. I guess my friends heard it too, because they were looking at the guys. I looked at all the guys and they were looking back at us. They were all smoking hot, like there might be a waterfall in between your legs hot. A few were sitting at a table and some were leaning against the brick walls of a store.

"We should go across the street and talk to them." Claudia said with a huge grin on her face. Ayanna and Taylor nodded excitedly.

"We can't or we'll be late." I said annoyingly.

"Well the first 15 minutes is always trailers, so we wouldn't miss much. Please? Cmon." Ayanna was pleading.

"Fine." I finally gave up arguing with them.

We walked across the street and they acted like a bunch of horny middle schoolers that are ready to get a boyfriend. I couldn't help smiling because they were my friends and when they're happy, I'm happy. And also cause I was pretty happy to see these hotties up close. When we crossed the street I started getting nervous, like I said before. I have no problem talking to a guy if he starts the conversation, but if I have to start the conversation, I'm like a blabbering mess.

••

Kyle's POV

"Yo dude look." Clyde said nodding his head toward the hot girls across the street. "I would love to dick her down." Clyde started laughing and then all of us joined.

I can't say that I wouldn't fuck one of those girls, or all of them. They were pretty and they look pretty easy. We were all watching the girls and kept talking about them.

"Okay, so there's 4 girls and seven of us. That means we're gonna have to do some double teaming if you know what I mean." Jacob winked and laughed and so did the rest of them. Me? I wasn't laughing because when I fuck someone, I want them all to myself.

The girls huddled on the other side of the street and looked like they were arguing about something. I wonder what they were talking about.

"Aye guys, look. You think they're talking about who they want to fuck?" Jacob asked.

"Calm down. You all know that the girls are gonna be all over me." Clyde said. He was really cocky, but girls did love Clyde. But not as much as they loved me.

They started walking towards us and all the guys started smiling and tried looking cool. I don't need to try to act cool or whatever the fuck they were doing cause I know these girls are going to want me. But my eyes caught one girl. She was walking behind the three other ones. She was short but she had everything I wanted. Like a vagina and an asshole, and a mouth. Just a few things that the girls I'm with need to have. They walked over to us and waved and said hey.

"Hey!" One of the girls said, she was skinny and had long wavy brown hair.

"What's up pretty thang?" Victor said with a smile.

The girl that said hey before started blushing and smiling cheekily. "Um, nothing much. We just wanted to come over and say hi." I rolled my eyes, because I knew she was lying.

Victor grabbed her wrist and pulled her towards him. And they started talking and laughing. My eyes were still focused on the shy girl. I don't know why I was so intrigued, because I usually go for the outgoing and easy types of girls.

"That girl over there is Claudia." A girl with curly hair pointed to the girl with Victor. "I'm Taylor." She smiled. "This is Ayanna." She pointed to the girl next to her. And Ayanna flipped her hair. "And this is..." She looked beside her and then she looked behind herself. She pulled the shy girl from behind. "And this is my best friend Ashley." Ashley was the one I was eyeing. She had nice tits and a beautiful face. She was biting her lip and her eyes were going from guy to guy.

The guys went up to them and introduced themselves. "So what movie are you ladies going to?" I asked.

Taylor nudged Ashley with her elbow and Ashley looked up hesitantly. "Oh. Umm. We're going to go see... Uhh."

Could this girl take any longer. Like damn.

"Suicide Squad." Ashley said and she looked at me. Well finally. I mean, what took her so long to speak.

"Aye Kyle, we should go see that." Clyde said. The other guys were talking to all the girls even Ashley. I looked at Clyde who was talking to Ashley, I saw Ashley look at me.

"Fine." I said with an annoyed expression. The guys went nuts. We headed towards the theatre. Clyde rested his arm on top of Ashley's shoulders as they walked. And I followed behind, you can guess what I was doing. If not then, I was looking at their butts. Not the guys butts! I was looking at the girl's butts. Taylor had a nice butt, it wasn't too big or small. I would love to get a hold of that. Ayanna had a very small butt and so did Claudia. What really surprised me was that Ashley had the best butt of them all. It swayed with her and it wasn't saggy. I really want to spank that booty.

When we got inside, it was pretty crowded and we still needed to buy our tickets.

"You guys are on your own. I'm not buying your tickets." I had to raise my voice so they would all hear me. Clyde was flirting with Ashley and it looked as if Ashley was returning the favor. Something deep inside of me was burning. Like I was angry that they were flirting. But why would I be angry, I've never cared what a girl has or hasn't done before having sex with me, as long as she doesn't have an STD.

All the guys bought their tickets and so did I. When we walked into the actual theatre where the screen was, I looked for my seat. I just want to sit down, kick my feet up and watch this movie. A few of the guys and girls went to concessions and I had asked Victor to buy my some popcorn and all he did was nod. I hope macho man brings me my popcorn. There were a few more trailers and the movie was about to start.

They all came and looked for their seats and sat down. Ashley and Clyde came in together. I guess Ashley wanted to sit next to Clyde, because when she looked at her ticket she looked disappointed. She walked down to where I was sitting and sat next to me. I looked at her facial features and the other features.

By the end of the movie, I knew that I needed her. I needed to fuck Ashley. I don't know why, but I need to. When we got outside I was going to see if I could smash.

"Aye! Ashley is it?" I pointed to her. I acted like I didn't know her name and I know she doesn't know mine. She turned around and nodded.

I walked up to her and wrapped my arm around her. "You should come back to my place and we can do a little something something. If you know what I mean." I winked and gave her my award winning smile.

"You nasty bastard. Ugh" She scoffed. She pushed me away and stormed off. Her friends looked at me, then at all the guys and ran off after their friend.

I can't believe she rejected my offer though. Whenever I do that, I have girls falling at my feet. Wait, no, I always have girls falling at my feet. So why was she different. Why didn't she want to go to pound town?

No. I'm not accepting her rejection. I haven't been rejected in a long time and I'm definitely not going to start now. I'm going to make that Ashley girl regret it. I'm going to make her beg for me to fuck her.

(A/N) I tried to make the chapter a little longer, so I hoped you enjoy.

Remember to vote and comment. Thank you loves.

(4) Jerk Face

Ashley's POV

After I dropped Ayanna and Claudia off, I drove back home with Taylor since she was spending to night at my house. I was still in a bad mood when I got home and the girls didn't try to force me to talk about what happened, which I was thankful for. When we got to my house we went to my room and I plopped on the bed.

"I call dibs on showering first." Taylor shouted as she walked into my room and grabbed her stuff. She smiled and left.

I sat up on my bed and went on my phone. I scrolled through Instagram and liked a few people's posts. Then I went onto snapchat and responded to people. I looked at how many views I got on my story. I'm pretty surprised, I got 153 views on one video. I put my phone down since I was in somewhat of a better mood. I still couldn't shake off what that guy said to me.

"You should come back to my place and we could do a little something something." Then he winked. That's the reason I hate guys. All they see girls as are sluts who will let you go in between their legs whenever you tell them to open. But we're not, well most of us anyway.

"Whatcha thinkin' about?" Taylor walked in. Her curly hair was wet and she had her pajamas on. I snapped out of it and smiled.

"Oh nothing." I shrugged to make her get off my back. It didn't work. She raised an eyebrow in a questioning manner.

"It's more than nothing. Hmmmm. Are you thinking about what that guy said to you?" She jumped onto my bed.

"Yes!" I shouted and tossed my hand up. "Those are the types of guys I stay away from. He thought of me as some type of girl that would just let him have sex with. Like no. I have morals ya know." I spoke loud and fast.

"That's true. That was rude, but he was definitely hot." She smirked. "Wouldn't you let him smash, or at least weren't you thinking about it." She stuck out her tongue and looked behind her shoulder.

"Hell no! I don't care if he had the biggest dick in the world and knew how to use it. I don't care if he came like a fucking hose and was the hottest guy in the world. I would never let a guy like him do the nasty with me." I sounded disgusted, and that because I was.

"Well I would let his friend, Dylan hit it. He was hot." She smiled. I gave her a questionable look.

"Aren't you trying to get with a guy named Joseph?"

She rolled her eyes and I laughed. "I was stalking his page, and I noticed this girl that was constantly commenting on his photos. So I looked at her page and she literally rides his dick." I started to laugh. "No she's like "omg he's so hot and he plays soccer." Or she'll post a picture of them together and said "had the best day with him ". But when I looked at both of their bios, they were both single. So yes. She's a kiss ass, or a dick rider." She crossed her arms.

I couldn't contain my laughter and I rolled around on my bed and accidentally fell off.

"Ouch." Taylor started laughing and I joined her. I got up and jumped back onto the bed.

"Anyway... What's that guy's name?" Taylor asked with a smile.

I looked at her with a deadpan facial expression. "His name is probably Jerk Face for all I know or care. Why?" My eyebrows furrowed.

"No reason." She smiled a devious smile. "Uhh. This random person just texted me." I looked at her. Then she showed me the text. "What should I say?"

"Did you give any of those guys your number." She started to think about it, then a smile came across her face.

"Oh yeah. I gave Dylan my number, and when he was gonna give me his number someone decided to yell." She rolled her eyes and looked at me.

"Hmmm. I wonder who it was." I laughed.

"Yeah I wonder!" We started laughing together. "Wait a minute, you guys are gonna do the nasty?" Taylor nodded in response. "But you barely know him." I said trying to make a point.

"Yeah, but he's hot and I'm pretty sure he has a big dick." She winked and smiled. Just like Jerk Face. "C'mon Ash, you know me. I like having sex. With hot guys."

"Ughh. Okay okay, but remember to be safe. And don't fall in love with him. He seems like the type to go around sleeping with girls." I crossed my arms knowing I lost.

"I know. I've done it like 4 times before." She shrugged as if it was nothing. I knew she was a slut and she knew she was a slut. But she's my best friend, my best friend happens to like sleeping with people.

"Nasty. Just ask him where do you guys wanna meet up before going to his house and getting it on." She nodded and got to typing on her phone.

•••

Kyle's POV

We all piled into 2 cars. I had my White Grand Cherokee Jeep. And Victor had his Dark Grey Aston Martin Rapide S. We sped out of the parking lot and we needed to get back to the warehouse.

"Yo dude what happened with that girl?" Chase asked. He was sitting in the back seat next to Nathan. I looked up at the rear view mirror and gave him an annoyed look.

"Nothing happened!" I shouted. I was pissed. A girl hasn't rejected me since sophomore year of high school, and I'm not breaking my streak now. Nathan and Chase looked surprised and didn't keep poking at the subject.

Wait, why am I going crazy over this girl. It doesn't matter if she rejected me because I get get another piece of ass anytime I want. I mean yeah, she's beautiful, curvy and shy. I really like beautiful, curvy people but shy women are too vanilla for me. Maybe I'm only into her because I want to turn her into a freak or release her inner freak.

When we arrived to the warehouse, Victor's car was already here. Everyone got out and walked through the back door. I walked to my office and logged into my computer. I had to read my emails about my restaurants. No surprise that business was booming and I was making a lot of money. There were a few problems at one of my locations. A manager was caught stealing food from the kitchen. The report was from the head chef who had to check inventory and found food missing. So he set up some personal cameras to see what was happening (which is a problem.) And he found that the manager was literally going through the kitchen and getting himself some groceries.

knock knock knock

"Come in." Damnit. It wasn't one of the girls. I could really some good top right now.

"Hey the guys and I were wondering if you were ok. Cause you got pissed after that girl yelled at you." Dylan took a seat in the couch that's against the wall.

"No I'm not okay." I looked up at him. I really was letting this situation get to my head which wasn't good. "I really wanted to fuck that girl and that bitch said no." I need her. I need that girl.

"Dude. You're pressed over some girl? That's not like you."

"I know that. But there's something about her, that I feel like I need. So I'm gonna need your help and some of the guys."

"For what? Are you gonna go to her house and kidnap her, because I don't think she's just going to leave with you?" Dylan said sarcastically.

I nodded and smirked. "That's not a bad idea. Go get the guys."

He stood up and looked confused. "You can't be serious."

"I'm serious, go and get the guys now." I was growing impatient.

He walked out and left the door open. Am I really going to kidnap this girl because she won't have sex with me or is there something else? All the guys came in.

"Really Kyle? I was in the middle of fucking Carrie." Clyde buttoned up his shirt and zipped up his pants. He looked pissed and I couldn't help but chuckle and all the guys were laughing.

"Is everyone here?" I looked over everybody. Then Nathan walked in and closed the door behind him. "Okay. While we were at the movie theatre, we ran into some women. Did anyone get their number or information?"

"Yeah, I did." Dylan spoke up. Thank God someone spoke up because trying to find this girl without any information would be hard. "I got her best friend's number if that might help."

"Yeah that's good." I looked around to see if anyone else got info. "Is that it? Everyone except for Dylan leave."

"So what do you want me to do?" Dylan asked.

"Send her friend a text saying something and see if you can meet up soon." I said with all seriousness.

"Okay." His fingers tapped on the screen and then they stopped.

"Sooo..?" I was growing impatient. Like seriously, how long does it take a girl to respond.

"She hasn't responded yet. Oh wait a minute." He read the text, then typed something. He walked over to the couch and sat down. Is he really sitting down right now.

I sat in my desk chair and decided to resolve the problem at one of the restaurants. I emailed the manager saying that I would be visiting in 2 -

3 business days. He needs to get fired because I don't tolerate stealing. I looked up at Dylan to see him smiling and laughing.

"What's so funny?" I said sternly.

"Nothing. Um. She said that her and I could meet up tomorrow evening." Dylan looked up at me without a smile.

"Are you going to her house or is she coming to yours?"

"She's coming to my house. Why?" He asked curiously.

"I need you to act really friendly with her so you can get her phone password. Then go through her phone and try to find out where Ashley lives. And try not to get caught." I said.

"Oh okay." He sounded hesitant. He got up and walked out the door. I need to plan how to kidnap her without anyone noticing.

(A/N) so I made the chapter longer and I'm pretty happy with it.

Please vote and comment. Adios amigos

(5) The Plan

Taylor's POV

What should I wear? Maybe go slutty. Nah, he would think I'm easy.

"Wear the turquoise body con dress." Ashley said as she sat on my bed watching me struggle.

"Ok 'miss I know how to dress and I'm good at clothes.'" I started laughing and she looked up from her phone.

"Hey! I am good at dressing myself. Thanks for noticing." She said sarcastically and she blew a kiss. We both started laughing. "Don't you think you're moving fast with this Dylan guy. Like you just met him yesterday."

"I don't think so. I mean yeah I'm moving fast, but if you move slow, then it's gonna take you forever to get where you're going." I said as I pulled the tight dress up. "I also haven't had sex in awhile and this cupcake really wants it." I turned and smiled at her disgusted face.

"That's nasty. I didn't want to know all of that. All you had to say was yes or no." I started laughing at her remark.

"I'm gonna wear white heels and I think I'm done." I went into my closet and grabbed my heels from the bottom. "Ok, how do I look?"

"Beautiful." She complimented.

"Ok so I'm done. I'm kinda nervous and it's weird. I've never been nervous before doing something like this. What if he doesn't like my body or what if I'm not good at s-"

"Okay stop." Ashley raised her hand to tell me to stop. "If he doesn't like you, then he's a bastard because you have a beautiful body. And being nervous is totally normal so calm down."

doorbell

"I think he's here." Ashley said sarcastically.

"Oh shit. I forgot to look to see if he texted me." I started to panic. "Uhh. Do I look ok?"

Ashley rolled her eyes. "You look fine, now c'mon, he's going to leave. And I want to go home." Ashley ran down the stairs and opened the door.

As I walked down the stairs I could hear them talking.

"Hey Dylan!" I said as I walked a little faster.

"Hey Taylor! These are for you." He handed me a bouquet of flowers. "You look very beautiful." He rubbed the back of his neck and smiled. Damn this guy is hot. He was wearing a white dress shirt with black dress pants and a red tie.

"You look good too." I smiled. Ashley hugged me and said good bye.

"Alright, you ready to go?" I nodded and locked my door.

"When I started walking toward the street, I saw his car and it screamed money. And when I got inside, the car was beautiful and clean. And when he drove, the ride was smooth and the car was quiet. We made small talk here and there and laughed every once in a while. We pulled up in front of a restaurant and Dylan got out fast and gave valet the keys. I walked up behind him and we walked inside together.

The restaurant was bright with chandeliers hanging from the ceiling and white walls. It was gorgeous. The tables had white table clothes with beautiful embroidered chairs. I couldn't believe that we were eating here.

The waitress at the front realized who he was as soon as she saw him. "Good evening Mr. Roberts. Your table is this way." We followed behind her and walked to the back of the restaurant. "Here's your table sir. Your waiter will be here soon." As she walked away, I stared at this beautiful man sitting across from me. I know we're only having sex, but what if we had something more.

"Do you know what you want to drink or eat?"

"No. It's all expensive and I don't want to seem like a gold digger. Do you know what I should get?" I asked sincerely. He smiled at me.

"Nonsense. You're not a gold digger if you want expensive food. Everyone gets hungry and we happen to be at a place that has food. The food might be expensive, but it's still food. So how do you feel about wine and seafood?"

"I'm only 18, I can't drink, legally. But seafood is fine."

"Just don't tell anyone you're 18." He winked at me.

****

After dinner we went back to his place. The atmosphere in the car seemed more lifted after we got to know more about each other.

"So before we get to my place, do you want to tell me what you like. Sexually?" I looked at him and gulped.

"I... Uh don't know. I usually do a little booty spank and ya know that's it. I guess all the guys I've been with has been vanilla."

"I'm not talking about what you've done in the past. What would you like to explore? Handcuffs? Blindfold, or a gag? Do you want me to be rough?" I looked at him with my eyes wide and my brows furrowed.

"Hmm. I can try handcuffs and yeah. I guess I would like you to be rough. But we need a safe word. Like apple pie." He chuckled when I said apple pie.

"Ok. Why apple pie? I mean, I understand having a safe word. But Apple pie?"

"Apple pie is one of my favorite desserts."

"Ohh. Okay. Sounds like a deal."

*******************************WARNING. SCENES IN THIS PART WILL BE VERY SEXUAL. PROCEED IF YOU WANT.

We parked in a parking garage for apartments. When we exited the car, Dylan grabbed my hand and held it. It was perfect.

"So is this where you live?" Well that sounded stupid. Of course he lives here, he brought you here for a reason.

"Yeah. Top floor." He responded.

We didn't talk or look at each other, all we did was hold hands while we walked into the building. He buzzed his fob to get inside the building and then we walked to the elevator. He let go of my hand and I felt cold, and lonely. I want his hand again.

"Can you press 12 please?" He glanced at me, then looked at his phone. I pressed the number 12 and the doors closed. I looked at him and he shoves his phone into his pocket. And in a rush, he had me pinned to the wall of the elevator and we were forcefully making out. I felt his hand move to my butt and he squeezed my ass then lifted me up. I was getting wet and craving his dick. Once we got to the 12th floor and the doors opened, he set me back on my feet and held my hand once again. The hallway was long and there were only 5 doors. He walked all the way down the hall and took a key out of his pocket. He opened the door and we walked into a dimly lit apartment. This apartment was huge and had a white, dark brown and gold theme. It was beautiful. I dropped my purse at the door and took off my heels. Damn, my feet are sore.

He picked me up again by surprise and took me to a bedroom. He threw me on the bed and undid his tie, as his eyes ravished my body. He smiled and leaned down and kissed me forcefully. His tongue grazed against my lips until I opened my mouth and let his tongue explore. Hopefully, his tongue isn't only exploring my mouth tonight. He walked away into a bathroom. I was about to sit up, but his head appeared at the side of the door.

"Lay down." He said in a demanding voice, all I could think about was following his directions. I heard a cabinet or drawer close and he turned the bathroom light off. He walked out with two pairs of metal handcuffs with red faux fur. My eyes went wide as he dangled them in front of me.

"It's ok. I'm not gonna hurt you. Unless you want me to." He smiled and winked. What is it with his guy smiling at me and making me all hot. He put the handcuffs on a night stand and undid the buttons of his shirt. He took his shirt off seductively slow and it made me even more wet. I could see the tattoos on his body and especially the muscles. He had a defined chest and his abs were mouth watering, especially because they lead down to his v-line.

He walked over to the handcuffs and picked them up. I was starting to regret saying that I wanted to try handcuffs. He locked my wrist into the handcuff, not too tight but there wasn't enough room to allow me to escape out of. He attached the other side of the handcuff to the headboard. He did the same on the other wrist and I was feeling scared now. Because he could be a murderer or torture me. I was roaming over his body with my eyes when I started to notice a few scars. There were lines, not stretch marks, but like he got stitches and what remained was a scar.

"It's alright. I'm only here to fulfill both of our needs. You need to trust me." I nodded my head. He sat over me, with his knees on both sides of my hips. He pecked my lips and his arms snaked around me until his hands found the zipper and he unzipped my dress. He got up to slide my dress off my body and as he did that ever so slowly, he gazed into my eyes and I really was starting to trust him. He threw my dress and just stood there looking over my body. I was starting to get self conscious, I felt as if he was judging my body. I had stretch marks on my breasts and the front of my thighs. The stretch marks on my thighs were very faint and only were on the top of my leg, but I felt as if they stood out.

I turned my head to hide my shame. "Hey. What's wrong?" He sounded concerned and grabbed my chin to force me to look at him.

"I.. I feel as if you don't like me anymore. Like ya know... because of my stretch marks." I clenched my jaw and felt scared.

"Trust me baby. You're beautiful." He said sincerely. He kissed my forehead and went back to taking off my clothes.

He kissed right above my underwear and slipped his fingers on both sides of my underwear and slid it down my legs agonizingly slow. I was getting wetter by the second and he knew it. He tossed my underwear to the ground and put his hands on my breasts. He fondled them and I guess he realized it would be hard to take my bra off, so he stopped. He walked into his bathroom and walked back out with a pair of scissors. My eyes widened in fear. Was he really gonna cut my bra, like does he even know how expensive they are?

"Please don't cut my bra." I begged and all he did was smile. "It was really expensive and..." He grabbed the shoulder strap and cut it, then he did the same on the other side. I frowned at him because bras are expensive and I bought this bra and panty set. He put the scissors down and unhooked my bra from the back and pulled off my bra.

"It's ok. I can buy you a new one. Depending on how good you are." He gave me a naughty smirk and I could feel my insides tingle.

He went to the foot of the bed and laid down in between my legs. He started kissing the insides of my thighs lightly and the anticipation was building. When he finally reached my vagîna he kissed it and got up.

Damn him.

He smiled and unzipped his pants and let them fall. Then he slid off his boxers, and his dïck sprang loose. It was big. Fortunately he was circumcised and his dïck was gorgeous. It was at least 8 inches and it was pretty wide. His balls weren't saggy and they looked full of cum. He only had a few veins on his dïck and the tip was oozing pre-cum. He went to the night stand and picked up a condom and put it on his dïck. I felt myself blush as I knew what was coming next.

He walked to the side of the bed where my head was laying. He got on the bed and hovered over me, well his dïck was in front of my face. I knew what he wanted and I was willing to give it to him. His dïck looked beautiful so why not put it in my mouth.

"Open up." He smirked and I complied. He shoved his dïck down my throat with a little force and I gagged. He started going slow, in and out my throat. He started groaning and I could tell he liked it. He wouldn't just stop before my gag reflex, he would try to shove his whole dick down my throat. Each time, a little more would go in. Then he started to speed up and I was really starting to gag. The tears were welling up in the corner of my eyes and saliva built up in my mouth. This must be what it's like to be rough, it didn't hurt too much, it was different. Him forcing his dick down my throat made a weird sloshing sound. He must've been close to cumming because he stopped.

He got off the bed and walked to the foot of the bed. He lowered himself on top of me and aligned his dick with my opening. He slid his fingers in my folds and fingered me. As if I wasn't wet already. I felt as if now I was soaking the sheets. He looked into my eyes as he fingered me and then at my lips. He kissed my lips with so much passion and lust. He kept fingering me and I could feel my orgasm getting closer and closer, then he stopped. He stopped kissing me and stopped fingering me.

He looked into my eyes for permission and I nodded. I felt his hard dick enter me slowly and it hurt a little. It had been a while since I had sex, but none have been this big. He slid all the way in and waited so that my walls can get accommodate his size. He started sliding in and out slowly, then he started to speed up. I was moaning and gripping the chains on the handcuffs.

"Damn, you're tight." He grunted as he started going faster and faster. I started moaning louder as I felt myself nearing toward the edge once again. He slammed into me and it sent me right over the edge. His hand was around my neck lightly choking me, which made my orgasm so much stronger. My vagina clenched and un-clenched. My body shook and I was a moaning mess. He kept pounding hard and fast, never taking a break. As my orgasm ended, I could see the sweat on his body. And the lust in his eyes. He stopped and got the keys for the handcuffs and un-cuffed my hands from the headboard. He took one handcuff off my wrist and instead handcuffed me behind me back. He pushed me down so that my butt was in the air and my face laid in the pillows. He re-entered my vagina and began pounding me again. He was grunting and I was moaning. His hand went into my hair and was pulling it.

A slap landed on my left butt cheek, then another one on my right. "I'm so fucking close." He said in between his grunting.

"Me too." A few minutes later we both were cumming. He unlocked the handcuffs and took off his condom.

We laid there, totally naked and sweaty. I felt tired so I closed my eyes and drifted off to sleep.

•••

Dylan's POV

Damn. Taylor and I just had some really mind blowing sex. I loved it. There was something about her that made me intrigued in her. She was beautiful and her body was perfectly shaped, her breasts weren't too big, and her personality is wonderful. But, being in this business, you can't catch feelings for someone. You never know when you're gonna die or if they might get taken and killed. So I prefer to just fuck them and let them be. The only thing that got me, is when I took off her clothing, she felt self-conscious of her body. I mean, I usually fuck girls with fake asses and tits and they look like a barbie because of all their surgery. So I never heard a girl complain about her body since high school. I just didn't want her to hate herself. Maybe she thought I fucked models and was comparing herself to them. I mean I've fucked models before, but some are too skinny for my liking.

Anyway. It was time to look for this phone. Taylor fell asleep and hour and a half ago. I had to make sure she was asleep before getting up and looking for this phone.

I remembered her dropping her bag when we entered my apartment, so I'll start there. I got up quietly and slowly so I wouldn't wake her up. I walked to her purse and found her phone, but the was password protected. But luckily, she had a fingerprint scanner. So I walked back to the bedroom with her phone in my hand and went to where she was sleeping. She looked so peaceful and delicate. Her hands were under her head, so it was pretty hard to get her thumb, but I always succeed. I unlocked her phone and went to go sit on the couch in the living room. I grabbed my phone or of the drawer from my nightstand.

I went through her phone trying to find any information about her best friend. I found out her last name was Rowens and that she loved food. I went through their convo and I scrolled until I found pictures of houses.

T- *picture of a house* is this your house? A- no T- *picture of a house* how about this one? A- nope T- *picture of a house* I'm walking to the doorbell. A- that's still not my house. You already know where I live. T- *picture of a house* oh yeah! It's this one A- yes. Now hurry up

Luckily I could read the house number on the picture, so I sent the picture of the house to my phone and then deleted proof that I sent it to myself off her phone. I looked up the house number in my area and there were only ten. So I matched the picture of Ashley's house with the pictures on the website and found where she lived.

I sent Kyle the address. I felt accomplished, but then again. I always succeed. I put Taylor's phone back in her purse and went back to the bedroom. I got in bed behind her and we were spooning. I snaked my arm around her and kissed her neck and I was off to sleep.

(A/N) I finally made a good long chapter. I feel just like Dylan, accomplished.

I hoped you liked it. Don't forget to vote and comment. Ciao!

(6) Knock Knock

K yle's POV

Thank God Dylan got Ashley's house address 2 nights ago. Now I have to find out how to get her. Am I going to do the kidnapping, is someone gonna convince her to go somewhere or will they kidnap her for me? Hmm. Gotta plan this one. I also have to get my pent house ready so she can't escape.

knock knock knock

"Come in." I said while pushing the thought of kidnapping Ashley to the back of my head.

"Hello sir. Are you still going to fly to Los Angeles tonight?" Sam asked. He was in charge of my schedule and getting things ready for me.

"No cancel my flight." He nodded in response. "Do I have anything else scheduled tonight?"

"Yeah. Cristina wanted to go out for dinner, then I guess she was planning on going back to your place." Cristina was a girl I used to fuck on occasion, but I realized she only wanted my money, so I dropped her. I still have sex with her once in a while.

"Tell her I can't make it." He nodded again and typed something into his iPad.

"Is that all sir?" I nodded in response and he closed the door and left. I got up from my chair and left my office. I knew the perfect guy to kidnap Ashley. He was strong enough to lift her, but he would be gentle to her.

I had to find Emilio. I went to the front of the club where we had our lounge and couldn't find him, so I decided to knock on all the private rooms. We only have private rooms to fuck some of the girls we own and for business. He wasn't in there either. Maybe he's selling right now, I'll just call him. He better pick up because I need to get this done tonight.

I called his cell and he picked up. Good thing he picked up cause I was getting impatient. "Hey Emilio where the fuck are you?"

"I'm on my way to the next buyer's house. Why?"

"Meet up at my house when you're done. We need to talk." I left a note on my door saying I went home.

"Uhh." I heard him gulp. "Did I do some-" I hung up. I walked to my car an unlocked it. I was driving my Jeep once again. It was a nice car and it could do anything.

I decided to take a detour on the way home and drive through Ashley's neighborhood. I drove past her house and parked on the opposite side of the street. I stared at the open front door. Why would anyone leave their fucking door open? Do they know someone could just walk in? But then people started walking out of the house with suitcases. Shit. They're leaving. Damn, and I thought I could get Ashley tonight, but they just had to leave. I guess their car was packed and they had everything. The beautiful girl I was going to kidnap stood outside of the door watching them put everything in their car. They all walked up to Ashley and gave her a hug and a kiss. They stood there talking about something and I wondered what it was. Like are they saying goodbye to Ashley? My hopes went up and I felt myself smile. Is Ashley staying home by herself? This is gonna be so easy. They walked back to the car and drove off.

I waited until Ashley got inside to drive off, so she didn't think some strange car was following her parents' car.

When I got home, I took off my clothes and decided to put some shorts on. I ate some leftovers and watched a few shows on TV. I heard my doorbell ring and I looked at the monitor to see who it was.

"Oh wow. Look who decided to come." I said sarcastically as I let Emilio in.

"Dude. The guy only had half of what was charged. So I told him that he owes me money for coming all the way out here, when he could've just called me. Then he said he wanted the coke, weed and ecstasy. He was only gonna pay for the coke, and I said he had to pay for all of it. Then he pulled a gun on me." I was pissed that this guy thought he could just pay for one thing and get away with it. Then this guy decided to pull a gun? If I were Emilio, I would've shot the guy in one kneecap and the other in his shoulder.

"... I was like. 'If you don't out that gun away now you little shit. I'm gonna kill you.' But he didn't put it away, so I shot him in the foot. He dropped the gun and bent over. So I told him if he ever pulls a stunt like that again, then he's dead. And if I don't get that money by next week, him or his family are gonna be in some serious pain. I also told him that it was an extra thousand dollars cause I had to put up with his shit." I was amused at the fact that Emilio shot him in the foot and found a way to make the guy give us more money.

"How much money does he owe us?" I asked.

"Umm." Emilio pulled out his phone and I guess he was calculating it or looking in his notes. "He owes us 17,000 dollars." I clenched my jaw, I was pretty angry now. "It's because he hasn't paid us the last two times."

"Ok. Anyway. I've got a mission for you." He looked confused, so I motioned him to follow me. We went to my office and he stood beside my desk. "I need you to go to this address and get this girl." I handed him a picture of Ashley.

"Why?" He looked up from the picture.

"It's personal. I need you to kidnap her. I have the chloroform and you can drive one of the trucks. Bring her back here and I'll take care of it from there." I handed him the address and some handcuffs.

"Am I getting paid for this?" He asked. I looked at him kinda pissed.

"Yes. You're getting 10 grand." He smiled and nodded.

"Okay and where is this night-night liquid?"

I went to my safe and took out out the chloroform. He walked out of my pent and I'm guessing started his mission. Now all I have to do is get everything ready.

I went to one of the spare bedrooms and started dusting and making sure everything was clean. I took out all the phones from the room and the bathroom connected to it. I walked into the walk-in closet and made sure there weren't any weapons that she could use against me.

● ●

Ashley's POV

There's literally nothing to watch. Disney channel has all these new shows, but nothing is actually that good. Ughhh. I'm hungry, my stomach growled in unison. I went to the kitchen and grabbed a tub of vanilla ice cream. I grabbed some sprinkles, chocolate syrup and a spoon and sat back on the couch. I looked at my phone and it was only 9:15. Thank God I'm in my pajamas, so I could at least just pass out on the couch if I get too tired. I was wearing no underwear, some pajama shorts, no bra, and a tank top that said I woke up like this.

It's cause I'm flawless. I grinned at myself. I opened the syrup and the ice cream and poured the syrup straight into the tub of ice cream. Then I added a dash of sprinkles and I present. The world's best ice cream. I went on to Netflix and watched Orange is the New Black. I had just started it a few days ago, and I am on Season 1, Episode 8. What can I say, it's really addicting.

After a few episodes, I peered at the clock and realized it was almost 11pm. I then looked down at the tub of ice cream and noticed it was halfway gone, damn I'm really fat. I mean I'm not actually fat, like I'm skinny, with a nice sized butt and nice boobs, my thighs are kinda big. But I'm not fat fat. I got up and put the ice cream back in the freezer and yawned after I closed the freezer. I didn't know how tired I was until just now. Well. Better get to bed.

I turned the TV off and turned off all the lights and started walking up the stairs.

knock knock knock

I froze as I heard that knock. Now who could be knocking on my door this late at night. Oh wait, it could be Taylor. Sometimes she comes over late at night and sleeps over. I checked my phone to see if I got any texts from her as I neared the door. I peeped through the peephole, but I couldn't see anything because it's dark outside. I'm so smart. I turned the light on and looked again, only to find a man standing at the door looking kind of impatient.

I opened the door and greeted him with a confused face. "Uhh. Can I help you?" I said as I held the door. Just in case he's a bad guy, I can slam the door closed and lock it.

"Yeah. I was looking for someone, but I don't know where they live." He itched the back of his neck and eyed over me.

"Mmkay. Who were you looking for?" I asked hesitantly. He looked up from the ground and grinned.

He stepped inside uninvitedly. "You." He grabbed a cloth from his back pocket and grabbed me as I tried to run. He pushed me to the ground and got on top of me. I was about to scream when he put the cloth over my face. I tried punching his face and grabbing at his neck, yet nothing seemed to be working. I raised my knee up fast and hard and heard him groan. He stumbled off of me and I scooted back and tried to stand up. He grabbed my ankle and pulled me back down.

"Where do you think you're going?" He sounded scary. I screamed again and pleaded saying that I would do anything to get him off of me. His legs were on both sides of my torso, preventing me from moving my arms. He covered my mouth and nose again with this cloth and I kept shaking my head. Soon everything started to get blurry and dark. That's all I remember before passing out.

••

Kyle's POV

phone rings

I walk over to my phone and check the caller ID before picking up. It's Emilio, I answer the call quickly after. Why am I so anxious, what the fuck is my problem?

"Hello sir." Emilio said.

"Do you have her?" I asked wanting to get to the point. I am really impatient and excited. It's like when you're a kid on Christmas and your parents keep taking pictures of you and your sibling descending from your room. And all you wanna do is open the presents because that's the best part about Christmas.

"Yup." He said popping the 'p'. "I'm right outside the building so, can you unlock your door?"

"Yeah. Make sure to take the service entrance and go up two flights before you get on the elevator. So no one sees you." I say sternly. I don't fear getting caught, I just don't want people to ask questions.

A few minutes pass. I've been waiting impatiently and pacing around. I sat down on the couch and groaned. What the hell is taking him so long. I should've done this myself. The door opens and I jump up. Emilio has Ashley thrown over his shoulder and he looks sweaty.

"She doesn't weigh a lot. But when you carry her up two flights of stairs really fast, it's like you're working out. Like training for a marathon or the Olympics." He complained.

I sighed and motioned him to follow me with my fingers. We walked into the bedroom and he plopped her onto the bed. I gave him a deadly glare and he shrugged his shoulders.

"How should we cuff her? Should we do hands, feet, one foot and one hand?" Emilio asked when he grabbed the handcuffs.

"One foot and one hand. Cuff her right hand and foot. So her dominant side is locked up. After that you can leave." I said. He tossed me a pair on handcuffs. I cuffed her wrist to the headboard.

"I'm not getting paid tonight?" Emilio asked as he cuffed her foot. I shook my head and glared at him.

"You'll get paid when that motherfucker pays us back." He nodded and said his goodbyes then left. I looked over Ashley's body. When I got to her breasts, I noticed that they look free. Like she wasn't wearing a bra. He breasts weren't saggy, instead they were perky. Ya know how people get boob jobs and their boobs be standing up on their own? Well that's what hers were like, but I doubt she got surgery. I groaned just thinking about it as my member started to harden. I resisted taking a peak, but I don't want to be a perv. But she wouldn't know I looked. I wonder if she's wearing underwear. Damn, picturing her without clothes is so fucking sexy.

Fuck. Gotta go jerk off.

(7) We Meet Again

Ashley's POV

My eyes fluttered open and a bright light shone in my eyes. Ugh. I closed my eyes and opened them again and wondered, where the hell I was. I looked around this ginormous room and I saw three doors and two ceiling to floor windows. There were black curtains on the windows, but whoever tried closing them didn't do so well. There was a small crack in the middle of each curtain where you can part it. Curtains are meant to keep light outside, not keep some of the light out, all of the light out. The walls were white and quite boring if you ask me. My head started pounding as I thought of ways to escape this room. I looked to either side of me and saw a plastic cup with some water. Damn that water looks nice as hell. I tried to sit up only to realize that my foot and hand were handcuffed to the bed.

Who the fuck did this? I groaned loudly and threw my head back on to the comfy pillows. I reached for the water and took a sip of it. If you're gonna kidnap me, you should at least put ice in my water because, who likes room temperature water. No one, that's who. I closed my eyes and replayed the horrifying scene from last night. I should've never opened the door. My stomach growled and realized I was hungry.

"I know stomach. We're hungry. We might eat a lot, but we're always hungry." I voiced my thoughts quietly. As soon as I said that aloud, I smelt the delicious scent of bacon. My stomach must've smelt it too, because it growled again.

I tried not to panic by busying my mind. I thought of all the ways I could escape. But I could only escape if I could get out of these freaking handcuffs. I groaned. Why me? No, why do people kidnap others in the first place? I hate people so much. I was soon snapped out of my thoughts when someone knocked on the bedroom door. Well there goes trying to play it cool. My eyes widened and my heart started racing. This is it. I'm gonna die and I can't tell my parents that I love them, or tell my brother that I'm coming back to haunt him.

The door opened slowly and a head peeked inside. I furrowed my eyebrows and tried to think of where I saw this person at.

He walked in the door with a smile on his face and must I say, my kidnapper was hot. But weird for kidnapping me. My eyes roamed his body. He didn't have a shirt on, so I stared at his toned body. He had toned pecs and a 6 pack. He was also wearing grey sweatpants, that hang dangerously low. His v-line was showing and I was admiring his sculpted body. I looked back to his face and it soon hit me.

It was him. Jerk Face.

"Good morning Sleeping Beauty." He said as if everything was ok. I gave him a deadly glare.

"You." I was consumed with anger. "You fucking bitch." I yelled. "Let me out of here." I thrashed in the handcuffs, trying to escape so I could choke this son of a bitch.

"I made breakfast." He placed the tray with my plate of food down on the bed. I had to stop moving or else the food would end up on the floor. He then walked to the nightstand closest to me and placed a glass of orange juice down. "Do you need any pain meds?"

My head was starting to hurt. But I didn't want to take anything from him. But I really have a bad headache. So I nodded. He left and came back with a bottle of Advil. He took two pills out and laid them next to my glass. He sat down on the edge of the bed and looked at my face. I was still pissed and scared. I was pissed that this bastard had me kidnapped and I was scared of what he might do to me.

He left the bedroom and came back with something in his hand.

"I'm going to unlock your foot so that you can sit up. Okay? Just don't kick me." He said as if he were talking to a child. He lifted the covers where my cuffed foot was and unlocked my foot. I was really considering kicking him in the nuts right now, but I soon pushed that thought away since he still had the upper hand.

I sat up slowly and he lifted the tray onto my lap. I looked at the food that was still somewhat warm. It smelled and looked delicious. I couldn't wait to dig in, but I also thought he poisoned the food. Even though that's a stupid idea. Because why would he go through the trouble of kidnapping me just to kill me? He could've gotten it over with. I picked up the fork and stabbed the pancakes with it.

"What's going through that pretty little mind of yours, Princess?" He asked genuinely. I looked up from my savory food. I shoved the piece of the pancake into my mouth and chewed slowly while glaring at him.

I chose to ignore his question. I dug into the food, and he sat there for a few minutes watching me eat. He might be hot, but he's still weird.

"When you're done just call for me and I'll come get your stuff. Then we can play a little game." He smirked and left. I started freaking out, what part of 'we can play a little game' sounds safe? NONE! What kind of game would we be playing, huh? Would it be a game where I run and he tries to find me, and when he does he'll kill me? Will it be a board game? A crazy game of truth or dare? I started to eat slower trying to figure out what kind of game we would be playing.

I finished my breakfast and slid the tray off of my lap. Here comes the thing that I least wanted to do. "HELLO!" I yelled. "I'M DONE."

He walked in shortly after I said that. Still only wearing those damn sweat pants. He smiled and I started freaking out. This is it. I'm gonna die. I knew it. He walked over and grabbed my glass and the tray and left. He came back and took a seat on the bed.

He sighed. "Do you wanna play 21 questions?" He looked at me waiting for an answer.

I started to think of all the possible outcomes of playing. I could find out why he kidnapped me. I could ask if I could leave. I could ask him what his name was.

I gulped and nodded. "Sure." He smiled.

"You can go first." He said. Does he ever stop smiling because it's weird.

"What's your name?" I started.

"Kyle. My turn." He took a few seconds to think of a question. "Do you think I'm hot? And you have to answer honestly." He said sternly.

I felt my cheeks get heated which only meant I was blushing or someone hit me. "I think you're a bastard, weird, and a decent cook." I wasn't gonna tell him that he indeed looked hot.

He raised and eyebrow. "You didn't answer my question. And I feel heartbroken that you think I'm weird." He said sarcastically.

"How old are you?" I asked.

"24." My eyes widened. He's that old. But he looks my age.

"What's your favorite food?"

"Mm. Let's see. Probably chicken nuggets and French fries from Chick-fil-a." I replied.

We started to warm up to each other. I still thought this guy was a bastard, weird, and good looking. I also found out that he's just like other people. It was our last question and it was my turn. I have been mentally preparing myself for this question. Okay, you got this Ash.

"Why did you kidnap me?" I said confidently.

•••

Kyle's POV

"Why did you kidnap me?" She asked.

Fuck. I was hoping she wouldn't ask. Should I tell her the truth or no. If I tell her why I kidnapped her, then there would be no hope for my goal. If I tell her a lie, there's a super small chance of me getting her in bed.

The lie it is.

"I wanted to become friends." I said even though it sounded more like a question. Hoping she would buy it.

"Why would I become friends with someone who kidnapped me? Why would I become friends with someone who thinks of me as a sexual object." She raised her voice and her face started getting red. I could tell she was angry.

"You don't have any questions left, so I don't have to answer those." I smiled to myself. Victory for me. "Do you have a boyfriend?" I asked for my last question. Hoping that she didn't have one.

She glared at me and shook her head. I know she's mad, but I'm happy. I looked at the watch on my wrist and sighed.

"I've gotta go to work. I'll have someone bring you some lunch later." I really don't want to leave. But in the business that I'm in. You have to stay on top, because if you don't, then something bad is bound to happen. Also because today I have a meeting with another gang. We are gonna join our families together and make one big family. Then we'll have more turf, money and more buyers. I got up and started walking towards the door.

"You're really gonna kidnap someone, then just leave? What kind of kidnapper are you?" She scoffed. Maybe she wants me to stay here with her. Maybe she wants me to help her relieve some tension in her lower regions. Too bad I can't at the moment. I walk out the bedroom and close the door.

I went to get my car keys and wallet out of my bedroom and check myself once more before I left. I sprayed on cologne and made sure I looked as evil as possible. I left my bedroom and I was about to leave when I heard a loud noise. It was like a crying noise and someone shouting, so I headed toward the noise and stood by Ashley's door.

She sobbed loudly and my heart was starting to ache. "Why me? Please.... please let me leave." She stuttered as shy cried and sniffled in between the words. "What did I do to deserve this?" She started crying louder and I really was considering staying here to comfort her. But I realized that she wouldn't find much comfort with me, since she doesn't like me. C'mon dude. Just walk away and leave. I convinced myself to leave, but it felt so wrong to do that to her.

(A/N) so I decide on doing short chapters rather than long chapters. That would allow me to publish the chapters faster and would be easier for me to write.

Who thinks that Kyle should've stayed with Ashley even though she doesn't like him?

Don't forget to comment, like, and vote for my book!

(8) Getting Somewhere

Kyle's POV

When I got to the warehouse, I walked in confidently. I noticed that there were more cars than usual in the parking lot, hopefully I'm not late. I walk toward the meeting room and open the door, only to see everyone in there waiting patiently. Some impatiently, but that answers my question. I was late, so I looked at the watch on my wrist and I was only 5 minutes late. Not too bad.

I walked over to Mr. Caito, to greet him and apologize for my tardiness which never usually happens.

I grabbed his hand and shook it. "Good morning Alonzo!" I tried to sound happy, but the expression on his face said otherwise. He looked mad as if I wasted his time. "I apologize for my tardiness. I had some..... stuff to take care of." All the eyes in the room were on us.

I walked to the other end of the table and sat down. Everyone sat down as I sat.

"Hopefully you all know why we're here today?" I went back to my serious and cold voice. Most of them nodded, I was starting to wonder why some of them didn't know why they were here. "Ok so before we start, does anyone want to speak against this?" It sounded like a threat. We started our meeting, at some points we were arguing and at some points we were agreeing with each other. I honestly didn't know what the outcome would be. Until 3 and a half hours later and we gave each other a document to sign. We read over it carefully, making sure no one was getting scammed. I signed the document and so did Alonzo.

"I'm happy you agreed to everything." I said. "Especially about the part of me being the leader and you being the underboss." I smiled evilly. Alonzo didn't look stunned or shocked.

"Yes. I read that." His voice laced with his heavy Italian accent. "Which is fine. It was nice being in control, but after a while it does get boring and stressful. So instead of me being stressed all the time, I can give myself somewhat of a break." He said as if he was some wise old man. Alonzo is only 2 years older than me. His mafia has been here for a while. His great grandfather started it as a matter of fact. I guess he talked about giving up control of the gang with his family, since his dad was also here in the meeting.

I walked over to shake his hand and thank him for his time. "I do want to make a name for our.... familia." He smiled and left.

Hmm. A name. I guess I'll have Sam arrange a name with one of Alonzo's men.

I walked into my office and sat down at my computer. I unlocked it and started loading money into everyone's bank account. Today's Tuesday and I had forgot to put money in on Friday because I was pissed off. After I was done with that, I logged out of my computer and went to the safe and grabbed out $50,000 in cash to put in my bank account. I locked everything up and I left. I told Sam that I'm leaving for the day and to tell everyone that I'm gone.

I looked at my watch and its 3:45 pm. "Shit." I muttered aloud. I forgot to get Ashley some food. I started up my car and left the parking lot. Pizza sounds good right now. Wait. She loves Chick-fil-a. Hmm. What did she say she liked? I kept thinking while I drove to the Chick-fil-a near my place. Oh yeah. She likes chicken nuggets and French fries. I love me a girl that can eat.

I pulled into the drive-thru and like usual, there's a long line. When it's finally my turn I get her some food and some food for myself and rushed back to my place.

Once inside, I walked quickly to her room and found her asleep. I don't blame her, she doesn't have anything to do in here. I shook her and she woke up. Damn, she's so adorable. Her eyes opened slowly and her lips part.

"What the fuck." She said groggily. "Oh it's you." Her eyes fully opened and she sounded unimpressed.

I sigh. I really felt bad for leaving her here. Here goes nothing. "I'll uncuff you so you can watch TV with me. But you have to promise not to try to escape. Because if you do leave..." I didn't want to threaten her, I didn't want her to be afraid of me. "You'll find out." I finish.

"Ok?" She said nervously. I took the key out my pocket and uncuffed her. She stood up and stretched. "Thanks for uncuffing me." She looked down at her feet.

She followed me out into the living room. She gasped and was in awe as she looked around. "This place is huge." She said. I smiled, proud of my accomplishments.

"Come over here before your food gets cold." I said with a smile. She ran over to the counter and her eyes widened in joy. A huge smile came across her face and it was lovely.

"OH MY GOSH! You got me CHICK-FIL-A?!" She was so happy. I just couldn't help but smile. She hugged me and it surprised me because after all, I did kidnap her. Her small frame against my large one. When she hugged me I felt her breasts push into me. I hesitantly hugged her back, but it ended very quickly. She grabbed her paper bag and her cup of Sprite and sat on the couch.

"I hope you don't mind that I got you Sprite." I said while walking towards the couch.

"Nah. It's fine." She was taking everything out of the bag. I walked over and sat at the other end of the couch.

"So what do you want to watch." I turned the TV on and started surfing through the channels.

"Um." She started to think while she chewed on her chicken nugget. "Well I just started watching Orange is the New Black, so we could watch that." She said. I gave her a confused expression.

"What channel is it on? I have all of them." She started laughing and her laugh was fascinating and the face she made was gorgeous. I guess she saw me staring at her and she stopped laughing and wiped the tears from her eyes. She gulped and looked at her food. I guess the fact that she's having a conversation with her kidnapper got to her.

"It's uh... On Netflix." She said softly. I went on to Netflix and searched for the show until I found it. We started from the very first episode. She looked up and started watching the show and I looked at her face. She looked scared, upset and somewhat focused. To say this show was weird is an understatement. In the very first episode, they had naked women. I saw booty and boobies. I liked seeing the two B's. I noticed that Ashley hadn't touched her food since she started laughing. She put it on the coffee table in front of the couch and sat cross-legged on the couch.

After about 3 episodes it was 6:10 pm. I looked over to her to see her still focused on the television.

"What's your favorite flavor of ice cream?" I asked her, breaking the silence. She waited a few seconds and I was starting to wonder if she was ignoring me.

"Vanilla." She said blatantly.

"How about toppings?" She bit her lip and it teased me. She started to think.

"I like... Cherries, chocolate syrup, sprinkles and marshmallows." I was surprised that this small woman could eat all that on her ice cream.

"Well I like pistachio ice cream without toppings." I said. She didn't ask, but I wanted her to know. "I'm gonna go to the store to get some ice cream and toppings. Do you want anything else?" She looked at me and looked away quickly.

"Fruit gushers please." She said quietly.

"Ok. But I'm gonna need to cuff you up before I leave. Okay?" I told her. I stood up and she stood up soon after. She walked into the bedroom and laid down. She looked sad and angry, but more sad. It made me feel weird inside. Like I was feeling bad. I cuffed her hand and said bye. I went back to the living room and cleaned up our mess. I threw the food away and our drinks. Then I left.

•••

Ashley's POV

I just laid there thinking. Thinking of how he remembered what I liked from Chick-fil-a. Thinking of why this guy that wanted to fuck me, kidnaps me. I think about where he works to afford a place like this. Then

I heard the front door open. Ugh. He's hot and yes he's somewhat nice. If he hadn't kidnapped me and he wasn't a dick head, I might have gone out with him. Then again, why would he date a girl like me? I'm ugly. I'm short, I like playing sports and sometimes I act like a tomboy. Why would any guy like him go for a girl like me?

The door opened and he walked in. I sat up, expecting him to unlock these handcuffs that hurt my wrist after a while. Instead he sat on the bed. He looked a little mad. Not crazy mad, but angry mad. Which was starting to freak me out.

"Before we sat down and started watching that show, you seemed outgoing. Why did you stop talking to me?" He looked up at me. His eyebrows furrowed and his blue eyes staring into my hazel ones.

The truth is. I don't want to get close to him. Why would I? He wanted to do me, then when I turn him down he decides to kidnap me. While I was laughing he was staring at me like a creep or... I don't know. But what I do know, is that I don't want to be here.

"Because you kidnapped me." I said sternly. "You have me locked in handcuffs and you stare at me like a creep." My voice was raised and I was starting to get angry.

He stood up abruptly. "I HAVE YOU IN HANDCUFFS SO YOU WON'T ESCAPE AND GO GET THE FEDS. AND WHILE YOU'RE CALLING ME A CREEP YOU'RE LUCKY I'M NOT CALLING YOU STUPID. WHO THE FUCK OPENS THEIR FRONT DOOR AT NIGHT TIME AND TALKS TO SOME STRANGER. YOU AREN'T EVEN WEARING UNDERWEAR OR A BRA, BUT YOU THOUGHT IT WAS OK TO OPEN THE DOOR TO A FUCKING STRANGER IN THE MIDDLE OF THE NIGHT?" He yelled at me. The fact that he was right about me being stupid hurt. I know I shouldn't have opened the door, but damn. Yell it in my face why don't ya? I was starting to wonder how he knew I wasn't wearing underwear. My shorts weren't even that short. My breasts must've jiggled to much, so that's how he knew I wasn't wearing a bra. This perv probably looked under my shorts or he... he...

"YOU PERVERT." I yelled at him. Tears were starting to well up in my eyes. Oh GOD please don't tell me he touched me, or raped me or took pictures of my coochie. His face turned red and be balled up his fists. If this were a cartoon, he would have smoke coming from his ears and nose.

"I'M NOT A FUCKING PERVERT." He yelled back at me and walked angrily out my room. He slammed my door shut and I'm pretty sure the door is gonna fall off its hinges. I was about to start crying. You know that feeling you get when you're crying or about to cry and it's like something is in your throat? Well that's how it feels right now. The thought of that monster looking at my no- no zone scared me. I was perfectly healthy down there and I was cleanly shaven but... No one wants to feel as if they don't have control over who sees their body. The tears started streaming down my face.

Now that I think about it, I'm pretty relieved. Because Taylor told me that when you lose your virginity, your coochie would be sore. Mine wasn't sore, so I now know that I wasn't raped, but he could've molested me or taken pictures.

The thoughts kept me awake, and so did the growling in my stomach. It must've been late since it looked pretty dark through the cracks in the curtain. I laid on my side uncomfortably and tried drifting off to sleep, but my bedroom door opened. I pretended to be asleep, so that the monster wouldn't start yelling at me again.

He came in quietly and sat on my bed near my feet.

"Dammit Ashley. I'm so sorry. I shouldn't have yelled at you. I shouldn't have kidnapped you. I wish I could do it all over again and be a nice guy to you. At the movies I should've acted more civil and gentleman-like." He whispered. I opened my eyes and shifted. Apparently he felt me move and looked toward my face. He looked surprised and tired. "Oh. Hey Ashley. Did I wake you?" He stood up. I shook my head. While I was waiting for him to bring my ice cream. I did think of one thing. It would be so much easier if we became friends. But after he yelled at me and found out I wasn't wearing anything under my clothes, I was starting to rethink.

"H-how did you know I wasn't wearing any underwear?" I asked hesitantly. I just wanted to get the thought of him touching me or taking pictures of me out of my head.

His eyes widened and I guess I took him by surprise. "Well when the guy that I asked to kidnap you brought you here, you were over his shoulder and when he tossed you on the bed, your boobs jiggled and it seemed as if you weren't wearing a bra." He rubbed the back of his neck, he must be embarrassed, but so was I. "Sorry about this but then I was imagining you naked and wondered if you were wearing underwear." I widened my eyes and my lips parted. I was shocked. He did look. Oh my Gandhi. He noticed my facial expression and started waving his hands in a shooing motion. "No, no, no, no. I didn't look. Trust me. I resisted looking, I didn't want to invade something private like that." He looked scared.

He left the room and came back with two big boxes of fruit gushers. That lightened my mood quickly. Food makes me super duper happy. "You got the big boxes?" I said happily.

He nodded with a small smile. He opened a box and I reached in the box and grabbed three bags of fruit gushers. He grabbed two bags of fruit gushers and put the box on the nightstand on the opposite side I was sleeping at. He walked over to my cuffed wrist and I watched him. He pulled a key out the front pocket of his pajamas and unlocked my handcuffs.

He sat down on my bed, this time text to me. I was a little scared. Like what if he tried to put his hand down my pants? Well then again, I'm not cuffed and I could always run away.

"So how did you like the movie, Suicide Squad?" He asked me. He ripped open the fruit gushers and ate one.

"I loved it. The Joker and Harley are goals. Even though they are crazy, they're so in love with each other. Like when he convinced her to fall into that hot weird liquid stuff, and he was walking away then he realized 'I can't let her die. I love her.' So he jumped in after her. Then he pulled her to the surface and then they started kissing." I replied with a somewhat long reply. Oh well. That movie was the bomb. "Did you like it?" I asked. If he says no, then we can't be friends.

"Yeah. It was pretty good. I feel like I'm the Joker and Deadshot combined." He made a gun with his hands when he said Deadshot. "I'm not crazy, I just do crazy things ya know? And Deadshot because his humor is the best and I'm goo-." He stopped. I raised my eyebrow while I stuck two fruit gushers in my mouth. He looked at me and smiled. I decided to just drop it.

"Well I think you're crazy and you do crazy things." I said as if I were stating a fact. "You kidnapped me which means you're crazy and you do crazy things."

We started having a good late night conversation. I guess we could become friends. That would help me get out of here a lot faster. While he was talking an image of my family appeared in my mind. Gosh. I wonder if they've called me and wondered why I didn't pick up the phone. Or maybe they had a neighbor check up on me. I wonder what they think happened to me.

"Ashley. Ashley. Ashley." Someone was waving their hand in front of my face. I snapped back out of my thoughts and smiled. "You okay?" He asked. I nodded in response. "I asked if you wanted to try to catch the fruit gushers in your mouth as I throw them to you?" I laughed. He looked concerned and probably thought I was bonkers.

"No. I'm really bad at it." I smiled. And popped a fruit gusher in my mouth.

"C'mon. Please?" He did a doggy face and I started laughing.

"Fine, fine. I'll do it. Under one condition. Can I take a shower because I feel dirty and stinky?" He nodded.

"Alright maybe you can stand up or get on your knees so it will be easier." He said. I was about to stand up on the bed. "No I meant stand on the ground or kneel on the bed."

"Ohhh." Was all I said. I stood on the ground.

"Here comes the first one." He tossed it up into the air and I tried to move my head so that I could catch it in my mouth. But to no avail, I didn't catch it. It bounced right off my forehead and he started laughing. I did a playful pout and he started laughing harder which made me laugh. When he was done. He tossed a few more.

Hopefully I catch this one. Seeing these fruit gushers on the floor makes me sad, because they should be in my mouth. He tossed the fruit gushers and it landed straight into my mouth. I started chewing on it and I was so excited. He started clapping his hands and had a huge smile on his face.

"So, you wanna take your shower?" He asked. I nodded and he walked out of my room. "I don't have women's clothing, but you can wear something of mine." He yelled. A few seconds later, he came in with a white tee, boxers, a towel and washcloth. He handed me everything and I walked into the bathroom. It was a beautiful bathroom. It had a bathtub, glass shower, toilet and a double sink. The mirrors were huge and it smelled like the ocean in the bathroom. I've been in here before, whenever I ask to use the restroom, but I've never taken a shower in here. I closed the door and started getting undressed.

****

I walked out the bathroom after I washed my hair and my body. I was dressed in the monster's clothes and they were ginormous on me. I walked out of my bedroom cautiously. I went into the kitchen and ogled at it some more. I couldn't help but admire this place. It was huge and beautiful. Why does one guy live in a huge place all by himself.

"I see you're done." He came out of nowhere. Probably not from nowhere, presumably his bedroom. "I didn't think my clothes would be that big on you." He chuckled. How I hate being so small.

•••

Kyle's POV

She was so beautiful in my clothes. My shirt ended right above her knees and my boxers were like long shorts. I looked at my shirt and realized she still didn't have a bra on. Fuck. Her nipples were hard and poking through the shirt. I wonder if she's horny or just cold. "Are you cold?" I needed to know the answer. If she's horny I could help with that.

"A little why?" She asked. I didn't want to sound like a perv that was staring at her boobs, so I just shook my head.

"Do you want sweatpants?" I started walking towards my room. I looked at her while I was walking to see if she was following me, but she wasn't. She was just standing there.

"No. I'll get too hot when I'm sleeping, then take them off. Which would be a problem because I don't have underwear."

I really want to give her those sweatpants.

She yawned. It was so adorable; her yawn was silent and she covers her mouth while doing so.

"I'm just gonna go to bed." She said while walking to her bedroom slowly. "Good night." Was the last thing she said to me before closing her bedroom door.

(A/N) hey guys. I hope you're enjoying the story. I just bought a box of fruit gushers and my dad took four bags and my brother took two and I ate two, now I only have 12 left.

Anyway... Be sure to vote, comment and keep reading. Ciao for now!

(9) And You Are?

Ashley's POV

I woke up and realized that my wrist wasn't cuffed to the headboard. Oh yeah. Last night. I guess the monster forgot to lock me up. I'm thankful for that because my wrists were really starting to hurt. I walked to the bathroom to brush my teeth and look at myself in the mirror. When I finished, I walked into the kitchen and noticed the TV was on. Why would he forget to turn it off? I walked over to the couch and almost jumped out of my skin. There was a guy sitting on the couch and he definitely wasn't the monster. He was smiling at me and let me just say that this guy was hot as hell.

"Umm." I looked around thinking that this guy must've broke in or it was one of the monster's friends. But the monster wasn't home.

"Good morning beautiful. You must be Ashley." He said with a smile which caused me to blush.

"And you are?" I asked. I was a little bit confused. How did this guy know my name, was he a friend of the monster?

He got up and walked over to me. "The name's Chase." He shook my hand and gave me a genuine smile. He was a little bit shorter than the monster and less muscular, but this guy was still hot. He had blonde hair and it was tousled but still cute. He had brown eyes and I wonder if he has a six pack, or a girlfriend. He seems kind and he's really hot. He spun around slowly and I was really confused. "Ya done checking me out?" He raised an eyebrow and I just gulped.

"Oh. Uh sorry about that." He chuckled.

"So you were checking me out?" He teased.

"No. I just got really spaced out."

"Mmhmm. Were you spaced out thinking of all the dirty things you'd want to do with me?" Let's talk about a big ego. Well you know what they say, he's probably compensating for something. I giggled at that and he gave me a questioning look.

"No. I was thinking about all the types of food you should be cooking because I'm starving." I smiled widely with teeth. He groaned loudly and slid his hand down his face.

"I can't cook."

"What do you mean you can't cook?" I put my hands on my hips and looked at him flabbergasted. "How do you eat everyday?"

"Well. I either eat out or have my cook prepare something for me to eat."

"How about when you were younger?"

"Either my mom or my sister would cook."

I reached for his hand and grabbed it. I tugged him a little and he raised and eyebrow, questioning my gesture.

"C'mon. I'm gonna teach you how to make french toast, scrambled eggs and bacon." I pulled him into the kitchen. "Did you eat yet?" I asked. He shook his head. I started barking out orders. I told him what we need, the ingredients and how long it would take. I also told him that he wasn't doing things right. For instance, he was stirring the eggs instead of beating them. How do you not know to beat eggs?

****

"I think we did a pretty good job." Chase said with a smile. I nodded in response.

We were sitting in the dinning room across from each other. I sprinkled some sugar on my french toast and he drizzled syrup on his. Everything was so delicious and I can't believe he helped cook. Luckily nothing caught on fire while we were cooking.

"So how old are you, Ashley?" He asked while chewing his food. Which is disgusting.

"Don't talk with food in your mouth." I scrunched up my face." I forked some food in my mouth while he just stared at me. I furrowed my eyebrows because I was confused what he was looking at. "I'm 18." I said after I swallowed my food.

"I'm 20. What's your favorite color?" Why is this guy asking me questions?

"Are you interrogating me? Cause I feel like you are." He chuckled and shook his head. "My favorite color is clear."

"Clear isn't a color." He replied.

"Fine. I like gold." I rolled my eyes.

"My favorite color has to be grey. Are you a virgin?" He asked curiously with a smile on his face.

My eyes widened at the very personal and weird question. "That's none of your business." I said. I tried to make him realize to drop the subject, but he didn't get the hint.

"So you are?" He smiled. I blushed.

"Nope." He widened his eyes this time. Probably because he was shocked.

"So you aren't a virgin. You're a freak aren't ya?" He was really prodding me about this.

"I. Uh. I'm a..." I looked down at my lap, I was embarrassed being a virgin, but then again I wasn't. I know that my legs can stay closed or open when I want them to. "I'm a virgin." I whispered. I felt the blood rush to my cheeks.

"Don't be embarrassed, beautiful. I think it's cute." He said, in attempt to lift the atmosphere.

He kept asking me questions as we ate and once we were done with breakfast, we knew a lot about each other. We put our dishes in the sink and walked over to the couch to watch some TV. I sat down first and he sat near me. I grabbed the remote and turned the TV on.

"What do you wanna watch?" I asked. Even though this remote and everything is a lot more advanced than normal remotes. He grabbed the remote from my hand and I looked at him.

"Hmm. You wanna watch something on Disney channel?" He teased.

"You betcha." I said enthusiastically.

"I was joking. It's because you're young and innocent." He stared scrolling through the channels. "Here we go. We can watch Deadpool."

After about an hour, I started feeling tired so I leaned on Chase's shoulder and closed my eyes. He wrapped his arm around my shoulders and kept watching the movie.

"You wanna go to bed?" He looked down at me.

"No. I'm good right here." I yawned and fell asleep.

•••

Chase's POV

Ashley fell asleep on me. To be quite honest, she's cute and the way she's sleeping on me is uncomfortable. Maybe I'll lay down on the couch and make her body lay on top of mine. That way her neck won't hurt when she wakes up and my shoulder won't hurt.

I carefully lifted her head and body off of me and slid my legs under her. Then I slid her body on top of mine and I accomplished my mission. I smiled down at her. She was still fast asleep, this girl must be a deep sleeper. I laid my arm on her back so I could rest it there and I continued watching TV.

She's so small compared to me. I'm 6'1 and she has to be at least 5'5. Her body is perfect, her butt is beautifully round and I really wanna touch it. But I don't want to do that, yet.

Damn I'm getting tired. I turned the volume on the TV down and I started to close my eyes.

****

I woke up and checked my watch. It's 4:57 pm. I was about to get up when I realized that there's a cutie laying on me. I looked down and smiled to myself. How does she sleep this long. She fell asleep around one and I fell asleep at around 3:30. I was about to reach for the remote until I heard the front door open and some footsteps. I bent my head back to try and see who it was.

Thank God it's just Kyle. He started walking over towards me. "Shhh." I held my finger to my mouth in a hushing way. I pointed to Ashley. "She's sleeping." Kyle's facial expression went from confusion to anger when he saw Ashley on top of me. I think he's jealous. I smirked.

"Take her to bed. Why the hell is she sleeping on top of you?" He whisper yelled.

"Oh. She fell asleep on the couch while we were watching a movie and I didn't feel like picking her up. So I just laid her body on top of mine." I whispered back with a grin on my face.

"Fine. Stay still in gonna pick her up and take her to bed." He put all his stuff down. And reached for her.

"No I got it. I'll take her." I sat up and put my arm under her legs and back so I could lift her. I stood up and carried her to the room she walked out of this morning. Ashley's pretty light. I tucked her into the bed and walked out to where Kyle was. "She'll be really hungry when she wakes up. We didn't eat lunch."

"Bye." Kyle was clearly angry and I don't know why. But what I did know was that I didn't want to get on his bad side. I walked out the front door and left. In the car all I could think about was Ashley. How she smelt like sweet vanilla. How soft her skin was and how beautiful she is. Damn. All the things I want to do to her.

I picked up some Chinese food on the way home for dinner. I was starving.

(10) At Night

Kyle's POV

I couldn't believe what I saw on the couch. After a hard day at work, I come home to see Ashley lying on top of Chase as if they're best friends or even more. I just wanted to punch him. Everyone knows that I kidnapped Ashley because I want to get in her pants and they know that she's mine. So why was Chase acting so comfortable with her?

I groaned loudly and slammed my fists on the counter. I went to my bedroom and laid in bed. You know what. I'll show Ashley. Hmm. Who should I invite over? Carrie is probably fucking someone right now and I don't wanna fuck any of the other girls. Ah ha. I'll hit up Cristina.

I dialed Cristina and the phone rung a little and then she picked up.

"Hey baby." She said into the phone.

"Hey Cristina. Can you come over tonight?"

"Of course!" She sounded excited. Her voice went higher than normal and she answered quickly. "Are we going out to dinner?"

"No. I was thinking about pizza and a movie at my place." I don't like spending a lot of money on her because she's just a toy for me. An expensive, annoying and Barbie like toy.

"Really Kyle?" She sounded upset. "I'm trying to eat healthy and you know that." I could just imagine her pouting.

"I'll order you a salad from the pizza place ok?"

"Ugh. Fine. I'll be there in 2 hours." She said then I hung up.

Alright now all I gotta do is make sure Ashley stays in her room but can still her then screams of pleasure and moans coming from my room. I walked over to Ashley's room so that I could ask her what she wanted on her pizza and that she'll have to stay inside her room tonight.

When I opened the door she looked as if she just got up. She was sitting in the bed just humming a song and eating fruit gushers. She's so beautiful and ugh. I feel bad for doing what I'm gonna be doing, but I want her to know what she's missing.

"Hey Ashley. What kind of pizza do you like?" I asked from the doorway. I crossed my arms and leaned against the door frame.

"I like the simple things in life." She smiled and looked up at me. Why was she acting so innocent and she seems like she's in a good mood.

"So pepperoni?"

"Nope." She said, popping the 'p'. "I like cheese pizza." I made a scrunched up face while she made a face of pure delight.

"Cheese is so... plain. The best pizza is buffalo chicken pizza. It's spicy and cheesy." I said. I was about to leave until I remembered she might want something to drink.

"Oh yeah. Do you want any soda?"

"Sprite please." She said innocently. I was really regretting this. But I haven't had sex since Friday. Which is weird for me. I usually have sex on Fridays and Sunday's and Tuesday's, and today's Wednesday. So I missed out on a lot of fucking opportunities. I walked out of her room and peered at the clock on the wall. It was only 5:30 pm and Cristina wouldn't be here until 7:00. So I've got time to kill. I turned on the TV and I guess Ashley heard it, because she walked out of her room and sat on the couch. She sat far from me, a lot farther than how she was with Chase.

"Whatcha watching?" She asked.

"I don't know." I said harshly.

"Oh." She whispered. She sounded hurt. She sat there silently fiddling with her fingers. After a while she looked up at me and she looked as if she was going to say something. Her lips parted and then they closed. But she kept staring at me. It was really annoying to have her staring at me like I'm the one that did something wrong.

"Why the fuck are you staring at me?" I raised my voice at her. Her eyes widened in shock and she looked scared. She stood up quickly and scurried to her room. I heard her sniffling and I didn't care. She made me mad by sleeping with Chase. Not intimately, but they still slept together.

I waited an hour before calling the pizza place to have them deliver two x-large pizzas and two large sodas. Now to freshen up a bit for when Cristina comes. I made my bed and put my dirty clothes in the laundry room. I made sure there were no signs that another girl was here, like hiding Ashley's ice cream at the bottom of the freezer and putting all the snacks I bought Ashley in the cabinets above the fridge.

30 minutes later there was a knock and the doorbell rung around my pent. I walked to the front door in some sweats. I opened the door thinking it was the pizza delivery guy, but it was Cristina.

"OMG I've missed you soo much Kyle." She screeched. She ran into me and gave me a hug. I soon started to compare her tall slim frame to Ashley's shorter and more curvy frame.

"Come in. The pizza guy should be here soon." I said. Now how am I going to give Ashley her pizza and drink when it comes. I sat on the couch, a few feet distanced me and Cristina. Suddenly Cristina stood up and sat on my lap. Both of our faces so close together and I couldn't help but wish that it was Ashley straddling me instead of this Barbie, Cristina.

Cristina stared into my eyes while I was trying to stare at the TV and ignore her. She put her hands on my face and forced me to look at her. She started moving her face closer to mine and boom. We were kissing. I didn't pull away, I started gripping her fake ass. She moaned and started grinding herself into my dick, talk about desperate.

She stopped kissing me when the doorbell ring and I pushed her off of me. I gave the guy the money for the pizza and a $20 tip. I closed the door and set everything on the counter. Cristina walked up behind me as I started putting my pizza on my plate and she hugged me.

"Did you miss me Kyle?" She kissed my neck. I was really getting annoyed. All I wanted to do was eat and talk to Ashley, but when I get mad, I make bad decisions and this is one of them.

I ignored her question and poured some Rootbeer in my glass.

"I thought you were gonna order salad." She said as she looked over the counter.

"Oops. I forgot." I said as I chewed the pizza in my mouth. I continued watching Orange is the New Black. Cristina came towards me with a glass of Sprite and cheese pizza. That was supposed to be for Ashley, not this bimbo. I couldn't yell at Cristina for eating or drinking Ashley's stuff, since she wasn't supposed to find out anyone was here.

"I'll be right back." I got up from the couch and she gave me a curious look. I went to the counter and placed 3 slices of cheese pizza on a plate and poured a glass of Sprite to bring to Ashley.

"When you're done, can you bring me another slice of cheese pizza?" I heard Cristina say. I was happy she was distracted by the show on the TV. I walked into the bedroom and put the plate and glass on the nightstand closer to Ashley. I looked at her sleeping there peacefully. I looked at her pillow and it looked damp. She must've been crying because of me.

I shook her and she woke up. I told her to be quiet and stay inside of her room. If she hears anything, just stay in here. She looked mad at me and sad.

I walked out the room and went back to the counter and grabbed Cristina another slice of pizza.

"Took you long enough babe. I was starting to think you forgot about me.

***Sexual scene ahead. Proceed with caution. If you don't want to read it, then skip the scene until you see more stars.

I looked at my watch and it was 11:38 pm. I tapped Cristina's shoulder and told her to go to the bedroom and get naked. I wanted to get this over with quickly. I put all the dishes in the sink and I put the leftover pizza in the fridge. I walked over to my bedroom and opened the door to find a naked Cristina laying on my bed. I walked over to her and she got on her knees while on the bed. We started kissing each other. I squeezed and smacked her small fake ass a few times, while she slipped her hand down my pants and started rubbing my dick.

She got off the bed and on her knees right in front of me and pulled down my pants. She started sucking my member and it felt good. I pulled off my shirt since it was starting to get hot. Her fake lips were wrapped around me and her mouth was making me harder. I grabbed the back of her head and started shoving my dick down her throat. I started groaning in pleasure as she was choking. I pulled out to let her breathe and she stood up. I walked over to my nightstand and grabbed a condom. I slipped it on and placed he foil on my nightstand. She walked behind me and I turned to face her. She pushed me onto the bed and hopped on top of me and started riding me. She was screaming and moaning. I was grunting and moaning. I wanted to be in control so I rolled over so that her back was on the bed and over her. I pushed her legs back and started slamming into her. She was screaming my name and moaning loudly. I know for a fact that Ashley can hear it.

After about 14 minutes of fucking, I finally came. I pulled out of her. I was happy to see no cum leaking out of the condom. She laid there there while I threw away my used condom. I slid into bed and my back faced her. I slept like a baby. Finally my balls got the release they so desperately needed. I couldn't help but think about Ashley as I drifted off to sleep. What does Ashley think right now, what does her face look like? Is she disgusted or jealous? I finally fell asleep.

****

Ashley's POV

I woke up this morning so hungry and still tired. I couldn't sleep while those two fucked like rabbits in his room. I went to the bathroom to use the toilet and brush my teeth. I walked into the kitchen and took out some pans. I was going to make scrambled eggs, bacon and pancakes. I looked around and noticed that I'm the only one awake. I accidentally dropped the last pan on the counter, I tried to place it quietly. It's my time to escape. I ran to the front door and started unlocking it. It had the metal bar at the top of the door (which was pretty high) and two locks near the handle. Once I unlocked the door I opened it slowly and tried not to make any sounds. I stepped into the hallway and looked for the exit. Adrenaline was pumping through my veins, I was finally free.

I heard someone clear their throat behind me and I turned around slowly. My eyes opened wide, scared of what the monster was going to do to me. He walked quickly towards to me and grabbed my wrist tightly. He dragged me into my room and I was stupid not to make any noise. I should've screamed or kicked or fought back. But I didn't and I don't know why. He cuffed me to the bed. My wrists and my ankles were cuffed and I was unable to move. He walked away and came back with a ball on some type of leather belt. I was terrified now. I was in shock and unable to move.

"Open your mouth." He said sternly. His voice sent ice daggers coming toward me. I shook my head no and tightened my mouth close. He pinched my nose and I realized I couldn't breathe. I was starting to freak out, so I opened my mouth and he took that opportunity and shoved the ball into my mouth. He released my nose and pulled the straps behind my head and buckled it. I realized I couldn't speak and all that would come out is muffles.

"Now. If I hear you make another noise. All hell will break loose." He said. I was scared. I'm surprised I didn't pee or shit myself. I was shaking and my eyes were tearing. I was so close to freedom yet so far. He looked at me like he wanted to kill me or something. "I don't know why you tried to run or thought it was ok to do so. But now there will be even more consequences." He got up and left.

I started crying. All the things that he could do to me. I was beyond scared.

(A/N) R.I.P to my fruit gushers because I just ate the last pack. Ugh.

Who thinks that what Kyle did was wrong?

Who thinks he was doing the right thing by getting back at her?

Was it even getting back at her though? Because I don't think she has feelings for him just yet.

(11) Your Fault

Kyle's POV

After I left Ashley's room, I heard Cristina's voice. I walked back to my bedroom and saw Cristina sitting up on my bed looking confused.

"Good morning babe. Where were you?" She asked me. Ugh I want her to leave. I don't have time to be messing around with her and deal with Ashley.

"I was handling some business." I said sternly. I scratched the back of my neck and she started crawling towards me. "I need you to leave." I told her. She stopped crawling and looked at me shocked.

"What do you mean?" She looked at me as if she was taken aback. She knows how I am and she needs to stop pretending.

"Call your driver or I'll tell mine to come pick you up. You need to leave." I started raising my voice. I was pissed off already and I wasn't in the mood for Cristina. She stood up and walked over to me seductively and used her fingers to trace up my chest. I looked at her and she looked at me with a smile.

"You don't really want me to leave. You've missed me." She whispered in my ear. I walked away and picked up my phone to call my driver.

"He's gonna be here in 15 minutes to pick you up. So be ready to go, when he gets here." I said. She stood there like a lost child. I really don't care how she feels right now. I don't care about anything. I'm just really mad right now because Ashley tried running away.

After Cristina left I made breakfast for myself and Ashley. I didn't want her to starve because then she'll never forgive me. I walked into her room with her food and drink and placed it on her night stand. She lifted her head up looking terrified and there were tears on her face.

"Eat." I said. I walked out and grabbed my food and coffee so I could eat in her room. "If you kick me, or try to escape when I unlock your foot, you're gonna regret it." She nodded. I unlocked her foot and one wrist then put the keys on a dresser. She sat up and grabbed her food and started eating. I watched her eat as I ate my food.

"Why did you try to run away?" I asked. Still pissed off that she attempted to run. She wasn't gonna get far anyway.

She looked up at me and swallowed the food that was in her mouth. "Maybe because I don't want to be here." She said with an attitude. I could sense the fear in her voice.

"Why don't you want to be here?" I asked. I knew that she didn't want to be here because I kidnapped her from her house. But I've been nice to her.

"I don't like having to hear people scream or moan at night. Or hear the bed banging against the wall. You kidnapped me when I would rather be at home. I have nothing to do here. And you're mean." She said confidently. She had a good point. I can't argue with her about not wanting to be here because if someone kidnapped me, I would've tried to escape. She started eating again and kept looking up at me.

"Well, I told you not to try to escape. And if you did, there would be punishments."

"What are you gonna do? Kill me? My family probably thinks I'm dead. Are you gonna spank me like I'm a child? Hmmm. Or you could just ground me. It's not like I'm stuck here all day." Spanking her isn't a bad idea. I could have her over my knee and lift that shirt of mine above her booty and spank her. I could make that ass red and she would learn not to run away.

"As much as I like spanking women. I don't think we're there yet. And I've handled your family." I said. Her eyes widened when I mentioned her family. Oh. She thinks I've killed them. "Your family is fine. They came home and found you weren't there, so they contacted the police. I handled it." I tried to explain what I meant by handle it. "Your punishment will be simple. You are to keep my place clean. Do not go into my room and if a door is locked, do not go inside of it. On top of that, you will be preparing my meals. If I leave late in the morning, I expect breakfast. And when I get home I expect dinner, unless I say not to make dinner. Do you understand?"

She looked at me with anger as she chewed her food aggressively. "Why did you have to kidnap me if you wanted a maid. Don't you see how big your place is. I know you have enough money for a maid." She raised her voice at me. I don't like when people raise their voice at me, but I need to try and seem calm. Even though I'm pretty pissed right now.

I sighed loudly. "I said do you understand." I was getting impatient with her. She nodded her head and continued eating.

"Does that mean I'll be without handcuffs throughout the day? Aren't you scared I might run away again?" She asked curiously, I could still sense the anger in her voice. I wasn't worried that she was going to run away, because

I have some of my men outside the door. So if she tries to run away, she won't get far, or even out the pent.

"I'm not worried." We ate in silence. Tension filled the room and all I wanted to do was become friends with her, or even more.

After she finished, I grabbed her plate and utensils and left without saying a word. I put everything in the kitchen sink and walked to my room to get ready for work. After I got dressed, I walked back into Ashley's room to unlock her handcuffs. When I unlocked her, she got up quickly and ran. I thought she was running away again, but I saw where she was heading and it was to the bathroom. While she did her business, I left for work.

•••

Ashley's POV

When I walked out of the bathroom, the monster wasn't in my room. I walked cautiously out of my room and took my time to look around the pent house to see if he was here. He isn't. Maybe I can finally run away. I put my pajama shorts and shirt on from the day I got kidnapped and walked to the door. I unlocked it and opened the door to see two large men standing in front of the door. One was tanner and more buff than the other guy who was white and had a smaller build. I got scared and slammed the door shut, and started locking the door. Shit, they're here to kill me. I'm gonna die. I ran to the kitchen and grabbed a knife, if they're here to kill me. Then I'm prepared to fight. On my way back to the door, I saw a piece of paper siting on the counter. I put the knife down and picked up the paper to read it.

The two men at the door are there to make sure you don't try to escape.
~The hottest of them all,   Kyle

What? Okay first of all, this guy is arrogant. Second off, how do you hire body guards because they obviously don't have ads everywhere. I sighed loudly and put the knife away. I walked to the door and unlocked it again. I'm bored, so why not become friends with your body guards. I opened the door again and they moved so that they were facing me.

I smiled and stuck out my hand. "Hey I'm Ashley. And you are?" The guy that was buff shook my hand.

"I'm Ricardo. Nice to meet you Ashley." This guy had some kind of accent. Like Italian or something. Anyway I shook the other guy's hand and he introduced himself as Wesley. I said bye and walked back inside the pent house. I walked into the kitchen and started my punishment which was cleaning. I cleaned the dishes we used for breakfast, I swept and mopped the floor. I cleaned the counter. Then I walked around the pent house looking for the vacuum. It wasn't in the front closet with all the other cleaning supplies. The pent house was HUGE. I walked into 2 other bedrooms and 3 bathrooms. There were walk-in closets and balconies. God damn, this guy is rich. As I was walking, I past by a door that was shut and I hadn't looked in the room yet. I moved my hand to the doorknob hesitantly. What if there are bodies or some kind of torture chamber. Maybe there's a red room of pain, like the one in 50 Shades of Grey. Yikes. I don't know how I feel about canes and whips.

I tried turning the doorknob but it wouldn't budge. It was locked. The freaking vacuum could be in there. I sighed loudly and walked into the living room, not feeling like cleaning anymore or exploring. I turned the TV on and sat on the couch. I was watching Phineas and Ferb, just when I thought I was comfy, my stomach decided to growl. I got up and went to the kitchen deciding on making a grilled cheese sandwich, since it's easy to make and it's fast. I grabbed the bread and went into the fridge to get the cheese.

Oh yeah. The guards. I went to the door and opened it. Like it was some sort of a reflex, the guards moved so they were blocking me from leaving.

"Calm down. I don't wanna try and run, just to get tackled by two grown men." I crossed my arms. "I just wanted to know if you guys were hungry, because I'm making grilled cheese." They looked at each other, probably questioning if they want to take my offer.

"Sure." The pallet one said as he walked inside the pent house. The tan guy followed in after him and locked the door. They sat on the couch and I forgot that it's still on Disney channel. I ran over to the TV and they both had grins on their faces.

"So you still watch little kids shows?" The tan guy asked. His accent wasn't very heavy, but it was there. I don't want to admit that I do. So I'm just gonna ignore his question.

"How many slices of cheese do you want on your sandwich? And how many sandwiches do you want?"

"I'll take 2 sandwiches and two slices on each sandwich." The white guy said.

"Make it like yours. And I'll have one sandwich." The Italian guy said after.

I walked into the kitchen and turned on the stove. Once the pan was ready, I melted some butter on it and placed two slices of bread on the pan. Once the bread was a little toasted, I placed two slices of cheese on the bread and waited for the cheese to start to melt before putting the slices together. I took it off the pan and, voila! I've got a grilled cheese sandwich. I made 3 more and turned the stove off. I served everyone their food and joined them on the couch.

"This is good." The Italian man said with sandwich in his mouth.

"Is this your first time eating a grilled cheese sandwich?" I said amazed. He nodded his head. "I took your grilled cheese virginity!" I smiled and his eyes widened. The white man and I laughed and we kept eating.

****

Gosh. There's literally nothing to watch. I should just go and take a shower then start dinner. I got up and looked at what there was to make. He had spaghetti noodles and meatballs. He also had frozen garlic bread and tomato sauce, so I guess we're having spaghetti tonight. I went to the bathroom and grabbed a shirt from the closet inside my room. It was a plain white t-shirt. I hopped into the hot shower and washed my whole body, including my hair. Once I got out, I moisturized my body and put the shirt on.

I started making dinner since it was 5:30 and people usually get home around 6:30 to 7, right? I boiled the spaghetti and started making the sauce and meatballs. I put some onions, pepper, and italian seasoning. Once the spaghetti was done boiling, I poured it into a strainer and kept cooking the sauce and started on the meatballs. I took the bread out of the freezer and heated up the oven. The thing I love about cooking, is when you're finished and you're like 'damn! This shit is good.' Then you just think to yourself, 'oh yeah. I made it.'

Once the food was finished, I covered everything and kept it on low. I sat back on the couch and continued looking for something good to watch.

(A/N) I'm not scared of thunder and lightning, but there's like a thunderstorm right now. And the thunder and lightning came at the same time and it was really loud. And I kinda got scared.

But if I were Ashley. I would've been like Beyoncé and sung Sorry. Because I'm not sorry for trying to run away.

Anyway. Don't forget to comment, and vote for my book. Gracias!

(12) Shopping

Kyle's POV

  I exited the elevator and walked towards the door that lead to my penthouse. The two guards greeted me and I asked them if Ashley had tried to run away. They both said she had stayed inside and even fixed them lunch. I was a little angry about them going inside and hanging out with Ashley, instead of them doing their job. I told them to go home and be back in the morning. I entered the pent and immediately smelled dinner. Thank God she cooked. I'm really hungry, since I don't have time to eat lunch every day. I walked past the dining room and kitchen and I heard the TV, so I figured that Ashley was in the living room and not in her room.

She heard my footsteps get closer to her and she looked up at me. She was sitting on the couch watching Psych. She paused it and stood up abruptly.

"Hello. Uh. Dinner is ready, if you're ready to eat." My eyes wandered from her face down the short length of her body. My shirts were huge on her which looked really sexy on her. I was confused to where my boxers were. I clenched my jaw after realizing she wasn't wearing boxers. She didn't have anything under my shirt. Her nipples were a bit hard, it's not cold and I don't think that Psych is something that gets you horny.

"Yeah I'm hungry." I said, trying to make myself think of anything else. I tried thinking of that bimbo slut, Cristina. It didn't work because all I would think of is Ashley. Ashley walked away and into the kitchen. I looked around the pent and noticed that she cleaned up a little. There wasn't much to clean since everything is always clean. I walked to my room and took off my suit jacket and walked out into the dining room. She had placed my food, utensils and napkins on the table.

There wasn't anything to drink on the table so I walked to my cabinets and took out two wine glasses and grabbed a bottle of Fox Trot Red by Fox Run Vineyards. The wine itself is really cheap, but it's sweet and I like it.

I placed the glass in front of Ashley's plate and her eyes widened.

"Umm. I-I can't drink wine. I'm not old enough." She said hesitantly. Her head was looking down.

"Well the law says you can drink underage as long as your guardian/ parent is with you. The guardian being me. And if you stay on private property it's fine. And I wish someone would tell me that I don't own this penthouse cause I'll beat them up. And you have to stay here while under the influence." I said with a smile, in spite of raising her hopes. She looked up at me like I was crazy.

"Why do you know that?" She said. He face was scrunched up. I chuckled and poured her a little bit of wine. I filled my glass half-way and sat down.

"I dunno. Sometimes I get bored." I forked some spaghetti and part of a meatball into my mouth. This is delicious. I chewed the food, allowing myself to savor the flavors. "This is very good! Who taught you how to cook?" I said with a smile.

"Did you think I was gonna make something bad? Anyway, my grandmother taught me how to cook and so did my parents." She said. I could still sense that she wasn't happy with me. She continued eating her food and so did I. I looked up at her, she's beautiful, but also a handful.

I watched her eat as I ate. She obviously had very good etiquette. She used her knife to cut the meatballs into smaller pieces and never once put her elbow on the table. Once we were done, I grabbed her plate and mine, with our utensils on top,and brought it to the sink. She grabbed our glasses and followed me. I washed the dishes, since she has done a lot all ready. She walked into her room without saying a word and I watched her backside. Her perky ass swayed as she walked and I was memorized.

••

Ashley's POV

I walked into my room after a very awkward dinner with the monster. I sat there just looking out the window. I wonder how many people have been kidnapped. I mean, some probably have it worst, a lot worst. Now that I think about it, me being kidnapped is a lot like those stories that I've read on Wattpad. The only difference is that I'm never gonna fall in love with Jerk Face, and I'm pretty sure he's not a werewolf. So I'm out of luck. Yes, he's hot and makes you question if you peed yourself or he just made you extremely wet. But, he's not my type. I like the ones that show you how much they like you by their actions and words. The ones that are nice and kind. The ones that you can trust. Jerk Face is anything but that.

"What are you thinking about?" I turned around to face the wonderful, Jerk Face.

"If I wanted to tell you what I was thinking, then I would have said it out loud instead of thinking it. But, I didn't." I gave him a nasty attitude and he deserved it. He acted like me running away was wrong. Any person who was kidnapped would try to run away. He pursed his lips then took a big sigh.

"Well. I wanted to let you know that you're gonna need some clothes to wear while you're here. So come into the living room and we are gonna do some online shopping." He said, then left out of my room. I walked into the living room and there he was, sitting on the couch with a laptop in front of him.

He looked up at me and smiled. I sat next to him, forgetting how he angered me earlier. I grabbed the laptop off his lap swiftly and typed in Forever 21 in the URL. I scrolled through their tops, skirts and dresses and added a few things in the cart. While I tried doing my online shopping, I found it very hard to focus. I needed music to aid me in my shopping. I went on to Spotify and logged in. I played my favorite playlist which consisted of Drake, Rihanna, Beyoncé, Nicki Minaj, and a few others. It helped a lot when I was shopping.

"I'm ready for you to buy clothes from here." I sat the laptop back on the monster's lap. He looked through my shopping cart and I guess he approved, since he didn't say anything. He put in all his information. I watched carefully as he put in his address and his name, so I could finally know where I was and who he was. He bought my clothes and handed me the laptop.

"You're gonna need some underwear, bras, toiletries, pants and I don't know what else." He reminded me. Next store I went to was, Hollister. They have the best skinny jeans ever.

He watched me search for jeans. I put a high-waisted pair a black jeans, high-waisted pair of light wash jeans and a few low rise jeans in the cart. Luckily, they were having their $25 jeans. Usually the jeans are twice as much. He bought the jeans from Hollister and I grabbed the laptop from him. The next store I went to was Fashion Nova. I got a few jackets and shirts from them. I also got two body suits. When I gave him the laptop so that he could buy my clothes, he scrolled through the list.

"What are these?" He pointed to the body suits. "Are they like bathing suits or something? Cause you're not gonna need any bathing suits."

"No. A body suit is somewhat like a bathing suit, but with different material and you don't go into the pool with it. They're very comfortable." He nodded his head and proceeded to buying my clothes.

He started typing something and I wasn't finished buying clothes. "Uhhh. I need the laptop back." I said. I looked to see what he was typing and it was the Victoria's Secret website.

"What size do you wear?" He looked at me. "In bras." I really didn't want to answer him so I didn't. He eyed my breasts then looked at my face. "Fine. I'll take a guess."

He looked at my breasts and kinda maneuvered his head so he could look at the sides as well. I felt very uncomfortable, so I crossed my arms over my chest.

"Do you wear a 36 double D?" He asked.

I shook my head and thought I should just get this over with. "Close. I wear a 32 D." He shook his head and looked for bras for me. It was kind of weird having him shop for bras for me, since he would never see me in them. Whenever he found a bra that he liked, he would ask if I liked it before adding it to the cart. I told him to stay away from the push up bras, because I didn't want too much attention to my breasts. He added 14 bras to the cart. Then started shopping for panties.

He first looked at boy shorts. I told him I wore a size large. I wore a size large because my butt is kinda big and I prefer not to have a wedgie. We got three boy shorts, then he looked at the lace ones and got two. I wasn't really a fan of lace. Then we got a few cheeky and bikini underwear. Then he went to the thongs.

"I would prefer if we skipped these." I didn't like thongs. One because the thought of having something wedged in between your butt cheeks is weird and sounds uncomfortable. Two, because I had no one to show them off to. If I didn't want panty lines, I would wear seamless panties. I watched as he put 5 thongs in the shopping cart. "Those thongs must be for you, because I'm not wearing them." I said. He turned his head and chuckled.

"And why won't you wear them?" He asked with a smile on his face.

"It's basically like having a wedgie all day. And who am I trying to impress in a thong?" I raised my voice, trying to get my point across.

He chuckled again. "From all the women I've been with, they've all wore thongs, so they must be comfortable. Why not show them off to me?" I was disgusted.

"One reason why I won't show them off to you, is because I don't like you." He pretended that what I said broke his heart. He winched and covered it. "Another reason is that, those thongs aren't for me, they're for you. Remember?" He laughed. And his laugh was a really nice laugh. It made me smile.

"I'm gonna buy them. Just incase one day, you do wanna show them off to me." He bought everything in the cart. He went on to Amazon next and bought my toiletries.

"Okay. So I need to... um.. buy those things for you. That you might need every month." He said hesitantly. I grabbed the laptop and got some pads. I wasn't a fan of tampons because I'm not mentally or physically ready to try and find a hole that has blood flowing out of it. I'm not really a fan of pads, because your blood might flow backwards or forwards and get on your underwear. I'm just not a fan of periods.

After we bought everything, I sang to the music playing and gave the monster a nice little concert. At the end of the Ashley tour, he clapped and told me I was a pretty good singer. He hugged me and bid me goodnight. I wasn't ready for that, so it took me a few seconds before I awkwardly hugged him back. We parted ways and went to bed. As I laid in bed and stared at the ceiling, I just imagined going shopping with my best friend, Taylor. Until I fell asleep.

(A/N) sorry that this took so long to update. I have a lot of homework now that school started.

I honestly wish I had someone to spoil me with clothes, money and food. My friend said to get a sugar daddy, but I'm not ready to give him any sugar.

Peace out.

(13) Friends?

Ashley's POV

It's been two weeks since the day I've been kidnapped. Not two weeks exactly, but you get the point. It was a Sunday morning and I woke up to the smell of breakfast and the sound of music. I hurriedly got out of bed and brushed my teeth. I can't believe I woke up late, I forgot to make breakfast. I walked quickly into the kitchen to see a topless man. I mean, he was so fucking sexy. The muscles in his back moved as he danced to the music and cooked. He turned his head, as I ogled his back.

Damnit. It's him. I mean who else could it be? This is his place. He smiled and didn't look upset at me. "Good morning Sleeping Beauty!"

I was confused to why he was acting so chill about me waking up so late. Because supposedly, I was being punished by having to cook and clean.

"Not gonna say anything back?" His back was facing me again. He snapped me out of my thoughts.

"Oh. Sorry. Good morning." I sat down at the counter and watched him silently as he cooked. He danced and sung as he cooked. I mean, he's an okay dancer, but a singer? I think he should get a refund on those lessons, cause they're not working.

I walked to the living room, because I couldn't stand anymore of the horrific singing. I sat down on the couch and turned on the TV. Oh gosh, I'm such a little kid. I went straight to Cartoon Network and Teen Titans Go, was on. In my opinion, I liked to old Teen Titans. I was addicted to that as a kid.

"Breakfast is ready." The monster yelled. I got up and walked into the dining room and sat at my seat. He placed utensils, napkins and our plates of food on the table already. "What do you want to drink?" He asked me as he searched through the refrigerator.

"Apple juice if you have it. If not, then orange juice. And if you don't have orange juice, then I'll have milk." I looked at my delicious looking food. He cooked pancakes, scrambled eggs, bacon, hash browns, and he even made a fruit salad.

He brought over my orange juice. I was really hoping for apple juice. He sat down and started eating right away.

"Did you sleep well?" He asked me. Thank Gandhi he had swallowed his food before asking. I nodded my head in response. I felt obligated to ask him the same.

"Did you?" He looked up at me and just stared. I noticed that he had food in his mouth, so I guess he had manners. After he swallowed he answered.

"Eh. It was ok. I had a very nice dream last night. But, the person in my dream doesn't like me too well." Was all he said. I was intrigued. I really wanted to know what his dream was about.

"What was it about?" I asked curiously.

"You're probably not gonna wanna know." He said. He sipped some coffee with a smile.

At this point, I was really curious. I was smiling and couldn't help but ask again. "C'mon, just tell me. If you tell me your dream, I'll tell you mine." He nodded.

"Okay but I warned you." He looked up, as to try to remember. "So basically. You were in my dream. You were laying on the bed, butt-naked and I had just walked in." I widened my eyes and he chuckled. I was kind of regretting my decision. "So I creeped up behind you and gave your ass a slap. Then you turned around and crawled toward me. After that we ended up fucking in all types of positions."

My face scrunched up. But not cause I was disgusted, more like I was confused. "First, why would I be naked. I have clothes. Second, why would I be on your bed?" He shrugged.

"I never said you were on MY bed. I said you were on the bed." He smiled and winked. "But if you want to lay on my bed, I have absolutely no problem with that." I scrunched up my face again, this time, I was disgusted.

"Ew." Is all I said. He looked confused.

"What do you mean 'ew'? I'm the hottest guy in the world." He pointed at himself.

"Yeah right."

"One day, you'll be like 'damn he's hot' and you're gonna want to fuck me. I'll be waiting for that day." He smiled. He picked up his dishes and brought them to the sink and I did the same.

"I would never think the guy that kidnapped me was hot, and I would never let you fuck me. I'm a virgin and I want the first time I have sex to be with someone I like. Not someone who I despise." He started washing the dishes. I watched his back as he did it. His muscles were mesmerizing.

"You'll like me one day. So what do you want to do today?" He asked. Not even looking at me. Hmm. That's a good question. For one I'd like to go home. If I don't go home, then I'd like to binge watch some shows. Play games, go outside. Hang out with my best friend.

He turned around and raised his eyebrow. I guess I was taking a long time to answer. "Let's play some games and watch TV I guess." I went to the couch and sat down. I never turned the TV off. He finished washing dishes and came toward the couch. I watched him as he walked towards me. His muscles make your mouth water and he was gorgeous, but I would never date him. He's a jerk, a kidnapper, a fuckboy and has anger problems.

"I don't have any games, but we can improvise. We could do 'Never have I ever', we could do truth or dare, we could play 'would you rather'."

I sighed. Thinking of all the games we could play. Then I got the best idea ever. "Can I invite my friends over?" I said with a smile. He looked down and shook his head. I guess the monster felt bad for kidnapping me. "Well do you have any friends?" I asked. He could invite his friends over. He looked up and smirked.

"Of course I do princess." He got up and walked into his room. He walked back out with his phone and sat next to me on the couch. I was having breathing problems. I know I'm not an asthmatic, but I felt like I couldn't breath. I have no idea what made this guy so breathtaking or intimidating, but whatever it was, it needed to stop before I die. He turned his head and stared at me while I ogled his body. "Would you like me to call my friends?" I nodded my head. I was unable to speak. I was close to his body, and it wasn't helping. He's a lot bigger than me, he also has a lot of muscle. He stood up and walked back into his room.

Snap out of it Ash. I heard groaning and yelling and wondered what the fuck was going on. The monster walked out of his room and came to me.

"Something came up at work, so I'm going to have to go. I don't feel like handcuffing you, and the guys aren't here to watch you."

It's my perfect time to escape. He's gonna leave me here alone, and when he gets back, I won't be here.

"So you're coming with me. Go get ready, we're leaving in 10 minutes." He walked back into his room and slammed the door. That was the perfect example of anger issues. I hurriedly walked into my room and into my walk-in closet. I looked through all my clothes and picked an outfit. I chose to wear a tight, white t-shirt dress. And my black converse. I left my hair down since it was wavy and I don't wear makeup so I was done. I sprayed a little bit of perfume on myself and I was ready to go. I left my room and there was Kyle. He was dressed in a tuxe. His hair gelled back and he had his gold watch on. If he was intimidating before, then this is 1,000 times more intimidating and sexy. He smiled when he saw me.

"You look beautiful. I'm happy I bought that dress." I blushed a little. We walked to the door and he turned and looked at me. "Do not try to run away, cause problems or get any type of attention. Do you understand me?" He looked serious and scary. I nodded my head and he put his smile back on his face. He opened the door and we walked out. He locked the door and we were off.

I took in my surroundings. This place was beautiful. It was a long hallway with just one other door, and there was an elevator. The hallway was decorated with flowers on small tables and paintings. We walked to the elevator and waited a few minutes.

Once we got on the elevator, I looked at the monster and he was looking at me. My eyes widened. "Just wondering if you were hungry." He asked.

"Could you tell by the way I look?" I struck a pose. He laughed. "I mean you were staring at me."

"Hey. You stare at me all the time." Oh crap. He knew. I blushed and scrunched up my face.

"I do not stare at you all the time. I'm just trying to remember what you look like, so when the police ask me to describe you. I'll know what you look like." I grinned.

"Why would you tell the police how much of a fun time you had at my place? Then you would describe the person who made your life better?" He covered his chest with both hands then pretended to wipe a tear away. "I feel so honored."

"Well I'm not hungry." I said and stayed quiet. We walked out of the elevator into the main lobby and there wasn't a lot of people. The guy behind the desk gave Kyle a look and nodded and Kyle did the same to him. What the frick does that mean? Anyway, we walked into the parking garage and found his car. Or shall I say cars. There was 4 of them and a motorcycle.

I looked at him and he smiled. "Are these all yours?" I asked in amazement and he nodded in response. He unlocked a white Jeep and opened the door for me. I awed at the interior of the Jeep and I fell in love. I mean, my Jeep is a lot better because it's the one I've always wanted and also because it's mine. He walked around the car and got in. He started the car and we were off.

"Thanks for not causing any attention. I would've hated how I would have to handle everything." He said sternly. We drove for 15 minutes until we pulled into the back of a club.

"Where are we going?" I asked breaking he silence. He looked at me and I could tell that he didn't want to answer my question. His face was hard and his eyes looked empty. He got out the car and I did the same. We walked into the club and there were men dressed in suits and scandalously dressed women. As we walked through the hall, people bowed their heads, as if they were paying respect to someone. But who?

We passed by a lounge area and the monster turned around. I almost bumped into him since I wasn't paying attention to where I was going, instead I was looking around.

"Sit." He pointed at the couches in the lounge. The couches were formed into a circle and in the middle, there were 3 poles. I sat down on the couch, following the monster's demands. Something about the way he said 'sit' and his whole aura made me not want to defy him. "Wait until I come back." I nodded and he was gone. I had nothing to do. There were a few women on the couch and they were looking at me. They looked as if they were gossiping, at least I wasn't the one fucking everyone to get money. I heard a door slam shut, so I turned my head to see the cause. I saw a woman and man walk out of a room. The man had a smile on his face and so did the woman.

I could only guess what they were doing in there. Doing the nasty. I guess the woman saw me staring because she waved and started walking towards me. She sat next to me. I could smell the sweat and something else. I guess that's what people talk about when they say 'smell like sex'.

"Hey. The name's Coco. Your's?" She stuck her hand out to shake. As much as I didn't want to shake a hand that was just used to do something nasty, I also didn't want to seem rude. "Ashley." I said as I shook her hand. She's really outgoing and beautiful. Her skin was the color of milk chocolate, her hair was black and in braids. Her eyes were hazel, her face was cute, and she was probably 5'8.

"What are you doing here?" She asked.

I don't know if I should tell her the truth or a lie, I mean I just met this person. "Waiting for a friend." Is what I said. Wait, did I just call the monster a friend? Her eyebrows scrunched together, I guess she was wondering why I was waiting for a friend inside of the club.

"Well let me show you around while you're waiting for your.... friend. You look a little bored." I gladly stood up, she was right. I am really bored. She walked all the way to the front of the club. To get there we had to go up a few stairs then keep walking. It was a really big club.

"Ok. So this area is the dancing and dining area. As you can tell by the booths, tables, dance floor and DJ station." She pointed towards the bar. "I'm pretty sure you know what that is." We started walking to the back of the club. She pointed towards the bathroom and kitchen. We walked through a curtain to another part. "This is the stripper area for club goers. Where I found you at was the stripper area for.... special people." We walked passed a few doors and then back down the stairs. She showed me around the "private area" of the club and I just listened. We saw a few of her friends, like Katy, Suga, Babydoll and Rosy. Once we were back at the couches we sat down and talked.

"Umm. Are you hungry? Cause I can take you to get some food." Coco asked me. My stomach growled as a response. She chuckled. I was hungry, I got to admit, but I just met this person. How do I know she's not gonna kidnap me? I mean I've been kidnapped once and once is way too much. Before I could respond, I heard he door open and men start to walk out. Some of them gave me dirty looks or ogled at me. They were talking amongst each other. I could've never been happier than to finally see Kyle walk out. I jumped up and walked towards him. Some of the girls and guys watched as I walked up to him.

"Can we leave now." I said. Feeling uncomfortable and hungry.

He looked down at me. His face looked cold and hard. But something changed. Cause he started to smile. He nodded his head, and walked towards the door. I followed him and we were gone.

Once we got in the car, he started it and just sat there. He rubbed his face with one hand and sighed. He looked stressed.

"Sorry about having to bring you here and I'm sorry for having you wait for a long time." I was shocked. He's apologizing. I buckled my seat belt and so did he. We went back to his house and he started making lunch. I watched him cook lunch for the both of us and something lingered on my mind.

I called my kidnapper my friend.

(A/N) I'm sooooooo sorry that this took me forever to write. Like you guys don't even understand. But I'm finally done with this chapter. I hope you enjoyed it and keep reading.

Adios muchachos!

(14) Weird Things

A TTENTION!!! THERE IS A SEXUAL SCENE IN THIS CHAPTER. JUST AN FYI

Ashley's POV

Weird things have been happening ever since I visited the monster's club. For instance, at the club, I called the monster my friend, to a complete stranger. When we left the club, the monster apologized to me, which he's never done to me before. We got Jersey Mikes subs for lunch that day and ever since then, we've actually been having a good time. I still have to clean the house and cook, but at night I like to bother the monster when he's watching TV or on his phone. Sometimes we'll watch Netflix or I'll silently watch him play video games. 2 days ago, he taught me how to play Call of Duty, Mortal Kombat and GTA. I honestly don't like Mortal Kombat because he never goes easy on me and I'm always losing. Then on top of that, he brags about it.

It's currently Monday and I've been kidnapped for 3 weeks, it dawned on me as I woke up this morning. I looked out the sliver between the curtains, just to see that it was still dark outside. I groaned loudly and laid back down. I wonder what Taylor is doing. I promised her that we were going to go to concerts this summer, but being kidnapped kind of ruined those plans. I went back to sleep, since it was currently 4 in the morning and I didn't have to wake up until 7:30 a.m.

• •

Kyle's POV

Damn. She's beautiful. I am currently in Ashley's room watching her sleep. Some of you might call it creepy or weird, but I don't care. Her hair laid so messily on the pillow and her arms in a weird position. The look on her face was so relaxed and calm. She looked like an angel. I glanced on my watch to check the time. I didn't want to be in here when she wakes up. 7:15 a.m. I couldn't move. All I wanted was to be in the bed with her. Our naked bodies tangled together from our previous activities. I imagined what it would be like to fuck her.

Would she like anal? Would her püssy be wet and tight, waiting for me to enter? The way she would moan my name would bring me closer to the edge. Or would her moans sound angelic? I glanced down to see my hand absentmindedly rubbing my growing erection. I need a cold shower. I walked to my room and did just that.

Once I got out of the shower, I smelt bacon cooking. My stomach grumbled. I hurriedly put some lotion and pants on my body. I walked out of my room to see Ashley singing to herself and swaying her hips. From what I could tell, all I saw was a big white shirt, must be mine. A smirk appeared on my face. I walked up behind her and grabbed her hips. She jumped and froze.

"Good morning Ashley." I said. She relaxed and bit. She turned her head around and had an awkward smile on her face.

"Good morning. I'm uhh... making scrambled eggs with our breakfast. I hope you don't mind." She responded. I could tell that my presence was nerve wrecking for her.

"Mmm." I licked my lips, and with my hands still planted on her hips, I started to sway. Just ever so slightly, side to side. She cleared her throat and I let go of her.

"Sorry." I apologized. I mean it was my fault that I made her uncomfortable and that I overstepped my boundaries. I sat down at the counter and watched her cook. She wasn't swaying her hips and singing a tune, just cooking. I mentally cursed myself out.

I ruined the fucking moment. Now it's gonna be awkward around us. All I wanted was for her to be comfortable around me, but still remember what I want. But now it's going to take a longer time. Nice going Kyle.

Ashley snapped me out of my thoughts when she placed my plate of food in front of me, on the counter. "Can you carry your plate to the table, please?" I looked up at her and felt like I was dreaming.

Ashley is honestly so beautiful, and kind. The way she said please really turned me on as well. Just imaging her saying that over and over, begging for me to let her cum. My dick started to harden. I must've been staring at her for a few minutes because she raised and eyebrow, in a questionable way. I smirked and nodded my head.

We sat at the table in an uncomfortable silence. No doubt it was because of my behavior earlier.

****

After dinner, Ashley threw away the trash from Chick-fil-a. She walked straight into her bedroom and that's the last I've seen her. Everything has been awkward ever since that stunt I pulled on her while she was cooking.

She wouldn't sit near me on the couch, she wouldn't give me hugs, she barely even talked to me.

I sat on the couch watching Stranger Things on Netflix. Her and I were watching it earlier, I know I shouldn't keep watching it while she's not here, but I'll rewind it for her later. I heard the shower in her room running which meant she was getting ready for bed. I continued watching Netflix for another hour and a half.

Thinking that Ashley was asleep, I could watch porn on the tv and jack-off. The tv is much bigger than a phone or laptop, and I haven't done this since Ashley moved in. I walked to my room and got lube, 2 of my favorite porn DVDs, and a towel. I put the disc into the player and sat back and watched. My discs were made by me, not that I'm in them. But that I made them with my favorite videos of porn. After a few minutes I was fully erect and took my dick out my sweats. Free at last. I added a little bit of lube to my cock and started running myself up and down. After about 10 minutes, I felt like I was about to cum.

●●●

Ashley's POV

I woke up to the sounds of moaning, groaning and screaming. Are you fucking kidding me? I got out of bed and walked to my door. I put my ear against the door and listened closely. It sounded like artificial moaning and screaming, like what you hear in porn. He could at least have the decency to do that shit in his room. I opened the door carefully, so that he wouldn't hear me. I was going to give him a piece of my mind for waking me up. I tip-toed out of my room and froze. I saw him sitting on the couch with his pants around his ankles. He was jacking off. His dick was long, thick, and had a few veins. From what I can see, he's circumcised. He started groaning louder which meant he was close to cumming. To be completely honest, this was turning me on. I could feel the area in between my legs getting wet.

He still hasn't noticed me. All of a sudden he started saying something that surprised me.

While jacking off, he started moaning my name. MY NAME. It was hot and sounded like something I wanted to hear often. I got some courage from out of nowhere and walked over to him. Maybe it was because this made me horny or maybe I wanted it to be over sooner so that I could go to sleep. I stopped in front of him and fell to my knees. He watched me with a 'oh shit I just got caught masturbating and saying your name' look. He stopped moving his hand on his erection and I put my hand on his dïck. It was warm, hard, thick and slick. I've never gave anyone a handjob or a blowjob in my life, so this was new to me. I started moving my hand up and down his côck, while watching his face. I wanted to make sure I was doing this right. I've watched porn before, so I somewhat know how to give a blowjob and a handjob, but not out of experience. I took a deep breath and leaned toward his côck. I licked the tip to see what it would taste like. It tasted weird, but maybe that was because of the lube. I put the head of his côck in my mouth and sucked. I swirled my tongue around it, hoping that it would make him cum faster. He started grunting and closed his eyes.

"I'm cumming." Was all he said before a warm, thick liquid started spurting out of his côck. I didn't know what to do, but I've seen pornstars let the guy cum in their mouths. When he was done, I let his dïck slip out of my mouth. He looked shocked. His blue eyes looked darker or maybe his pupil was bigger. On Wattpad, people wrote that 'lust' would fill their eyes. But who knows? I opened my mouth and showed him the cum that was sitting there. I closed my mouth to swallow it, while tasting it at the same time. It was salty, but really sweet. It was also thick. I stood up and walked away. Before I walked into my room he said something.

"Ashley? Do you want to-" I cut him off before he could finish his sentence. I turned around swiftly, and said.

"Now will you stop moaning and groaning or at least watch porn in your room while I get my beauty sleep?" I smiled and walked into my bedroom and closed my door. I sat on my bed and ran my fingers through my hair.

I couldn't believe I just did that. Not only that, but I did it to the guy who's a jerk and kidnapped me. What the heck is wrong with me. I went to the bathroom and brushed my teeth for the second time tonight.

As I laid in bed, staring at the ceiling. All I could think about was how good his cum tasted, how big his dick was and the way he moaned my name. I ran my hand down my body until I found that spot in between my legs that was aching for attention. I masturbated to the thought of Kyle's dick. After my orgasm passed, I realized how dirty my thoughts were. Where were they coming from, because 3 weeks ago, I would've never did or thought of something like that.

(15) Thank You

Ashley's POV

I woke up the next day feeling just like normal. The scenes that took place last night replayed in my mind. I still can't believe I did that. I don't know why I would do something like that in the first place. The reason is; I'm a virgin, I don't want to have sex with the guy before dating, the Monster is a jerk, he's also a kidnapper, I've never done anything like that before, nor have I thought about doing it. Well maybe the last part is a lie. There were plenty of hot guys at my high school that I would've given a handjob to, because they were hot and I like hot people. But they were all fuckboys, so that was a turn off. I walked into my bathroom and looked at myself in the mirror. I had a certain glow, like I put highlighter on my cheekbones. I looked refreshed. I started brushing my teeth and thought of all the ways to apologize for what happened last night.

I came up with 2 ways to handle this situation. First, I could say I'm sorry for invading your personal space and touching you inappropriately without your consent. Even though you never told me to stop. Also, I promise to never let that happen again.

Or the second option. Which was to say I'm sorry for what I did last night. It's just you we're making too much noise and I was trying to sleep. You're not supposed to mess with a girl while she's trying to sleep. I just wanted the noise to be over sooner.

When I realized that I had totally zoned out while brushing my teeth, it was already too late. I had gotten toothpaste all over my shirt and a little on my pants. I started to undress. I looked at myself in the mirror with only a lace thong on. I've never worn thongs before because they look uncomfortable. Even after the monster bought some for me, I still haven't worn them. But last night I put the lace ones on just to try it, and they're really comfy. Like it feels like I'm not wearing underwear. Anyway, I started to admire my body. I gave my breasts a squeeze and poked at my butt a little. My ass is really fat. Like it jiggles. I went to my closet and grabbed a crop top that said princess and some knee socks. As I put everything on, I heard music playing. I walked out of my room into the living room and it was even louder. It was coming from the kitchen. I walked to the kitchen to see where this music was coming from. I looked on the counter and saw and iPod and a speaker. I picked up the iPod and went through it. It was a beautiful iPod and had games and music on it. I searched for Beyoncé and started playing all of her best songs. I started singing and dancing around the kitchen while trying to cook. It was hard to get anything done, as I was dancing and singing my butt off. I didn't hear anyone come into the kitchen, because when I opened my eyes, I saw the monster. I was about to throw the spatula at him, because I was so scared. He was just sitting there, smiling at me.

"Good morning princess." He said. I gave him a slight smile and proceeded into cooking. I was quite embarrassed that he had seen me dancing and singing so..., dramatically.

"So I see that you've found your iPod." I turned around abruptly and looked him. He said it was MY iPod. My eyes went wide and my mouth opened in shock.

"Wait. This is mine?!" He nodded his head and smiled. He got up from the counter and slowly walked towards me. He was wearing basketball shorts and some socks, but that was it. I could see his morning wood poking through his pants , which reminded me of what happened last night. Just the thought of it made me a little horny.

"Do you like it?" He said when he was a little closer to me. I looked up from staring at his côck, with wide eyes.

What was he talking about? What do I like? His dick? "Umm. What are we talking about?" I asked hesitantly. He was now right in front of me, I could feel the tip of his côck poking me ever so slightly. I gulped and turned around. He was making me nervous and wet. What's happening to me? If he would've done this a few weeks ago, I would've pushed him off and called him a 'perv' but now I get wet and nervous?

The way his côck was poking one of my butt cheeks brought me back from my thoughts. I started mixing the pancake batter.

"Ashley, we're going out for breakfast. I'm starving and you haven't started cooking yet." He said. He turned me around, and smirked.

"Sorry." I said and looked down. He put his finger under my chin and lifted my head so that I would look him in the eyes.

"I need to thank you for last night. Come with me." He grabbed my hand and started walking towards his bedroom. I noticed that my hand fit nicely in his large hand. What I've read on Wattpad, it says that you'll feel sparks when the right person for you touches you. I don't know if it's sparks, but I did feel something. Oh Gahndi, I hope I'm not starting to like my kidnapper. I snapped out of my thoughts and noticed that we were inside of his room.

"What are we doing in here? I thought I wasn't allowed in here." I asked him before we got any further.

"Well it's a surprise. Lay down on the bed." I let go of his hand and stepped back a few steps.

"I'm definitely not having sex with you." I was about to leave when he grabbed my arm and pulled me towards himself.

"We aren't having sex. Just lay on the bed." I sighed and went to his bed and laid down. I laid across the bottom of the bed. Damn, his bed is bigger and a lot more comfortable than mine. He prowled towards me and got on his knees right in front of my legs. "Spread your legs." He demanded. I didn't know what was going on, but he was making me really wet and I felt like I should just listen to what he said. I slowly spread my legs for him. He leaned in and inhaled deeply and groaned.

"May I?" Was all he said. I was really confused, and I guessed it showed on my face. He smiled and chuckled. "May I remove your panties?" I was really nervous. I've never done anything with anyone like this. The only sexual thing I've done with someone was put my mouth on their dick and help them cum, and that was only last night.

He started by kissing the insides of my thighs and around the bottom part of the panties. He would kiss, suck and nibble and it was starting to drive me crazy. He got up a little while looking in my eyes and kissed the spot right above my thong. He got the band of the thong between his teeth and slowly tugged it down. I had to raise my butt a little so that he could continue. Once my panties were off, I was a even more nervous. He was back on his knees, just staring at my vagîna. He sniffed it and groaned.

"It's beautiful, it smells good, and it's wet just for me." He pulled me closer to the edge of the bed and had me bend my knees. "May I satisfy my hunger?" He asked before starting anything.

"Yes?" Was all I said and his tongue starting flicking at my clît. He was sucking on it, nibbling, and licking. Sometimes he would go slow and other times he would be going fast. I was a moaning mess. My feet ended up on his back and that's where they stayed while he played with my clît. Next thing I knew, he was sticking his tongue inside of me. He was swirling it around and flicking it. He took his hand off of my thigh and placed a finger inside of my vagîna while his tongue went back to playing with my clît. He added another finger and was really making me moan. Obviously he has done this before because he worked me well. His fingers were sliding in and out of me quickly and his tongue was working fast. I was so close to the edge. All of a sudden he slowed his fingers and removed his mouth.

"Beg for it. Tell me what you want." He smiled and moved his fingers very slowly. I could see my slickness on his face, and he could no doubt see that I so badly needed to orgasm.

"PLEASE." I moaned and arched my back. He chuckled.

"Please what?"

"Please let me.... cum." I said quietly. I bit my lip and closed my eyes. He dove right into going fast and doing his best tricks. His tongue was so talented and so were those fingers moving inside of me.

"I'M CUMMING!" I screamed. He placed his mouth over my entrance and sucked all the juices that flowed out of me. My body shook and I was in pure ecstasy. When my orgasm was over he stood up and eased my legs down.

"Have you ever squirted before?" He asked me with a smile.

I shook my head no, too tired to speak. He chuckled. "Well you just did. Let's get ready, we have to go eat. Breakfast is over, but the brunch menu should be out." I sat up slowly and got up. I was embarrassed to look him in the eyes. I don't know why though.

This wasn't supposed to happen, we weren't supposed to do anything like this. I walked to my room and got dressed. I put some black denim booty shorts and a white crop top on. I put my white chucks on and left my room. I guess I was taking a long time because Kyle was at the door waiting for me.

•*•*•*•*•*•*•*•*•*•*•*•*•*•*•*•*•*

KYLE'S POV

We sat outside at my restaurant. Ashley looked everywhere except for at me. I'm confused. I thought she liked that I ate her out. I definitely gave her the biggest orgasm she's ever had, so why is she avoiding me?

The waiter served us our food. Ashley started eating and so did I. I watched her eat and she cleared her throat. She still hasn't looked at me, she was staring at her food.

"About what happened last night." She said. Obviously uncomfortable with the subject. The next thing I need to do is make her more comfortable around me. "That can't happen again. I don't know what got into me, but I don't want it to happen again. You were just making a lot of noise while I was trying to sleep and I just wanted you to be quiet. So, I decided that helping you... Ya know? I thought it would make you become quiet faster. Which worked. Just next time, could you do that in your room?" She finally looked up. I was glad to see those beautiful hazel eyes of hers.

"Yes. Next time I will do it in my room. If you don't mind me asking, why don't you want it to happen anymore?"

She sighed. "You know that you..." she looked around. "Kidnapped me." She whispered. "I'm not supposed to like you for doing that. You took me away from my life. You forced me into your life. Also, I'm a virgin. I wanted my first time doing anything sexual to be with someone I like or even love."

I understood. She was never going to like me because I kidnapped her. She was never going to see me as a nice person because I took her.

"I'm sorry about that. But who said you can't fall in love with the person that napped you? Who said I was looking for love?"

"That's exactly why I don't want anything like that to happen. Because we are both looking for two different things. Also, I don't want something like what happened this morning, to ever happen again. Like I said before, I want that person to love me and I would love them back."

"All I was doing was saying 'thank you'. And since what happened last night is never going to happen again, then neither is what happened this morning."

She had angered me. I can't believe that she won't allow me to fuck her. Only people that 'loved her' can. I don't want to fall in love. I've seen what love can do to someone, and I never want that to happen to me. I called the waiter over and asked for our check. I needed to get away from here. From her. Before I let anger consume me and do something I'm going to regret.

****

"Kyle, what's wrong?" Emilio asked, sensing something was wrong.

I didn't want to talk to anyone, I wanted to beat the shit out of someone. I wanted to destroy something. I went into my office and threw everything that was on my desk around the room. I threw my computer at the wall, I threw things on the ground. I even punched a hole in the wall.

People walked into my office to see what all the commotion was about. They all looked shocked when the scanned my office.

"OUT." I shouted with anger. Everyone left except for Dylan and Emilio. "What do you not understand about the word OUT?" I was really pissed that they weren't listening to me.

"We're not leaving until you tell us what the fuck is wrong with you." Emilio said. Emilio was never scared of me, he was a big guy. Whenever we got mad, we would fight with each other to relieve the tension.

I sat down on my chair and sighed loudly. "Ashley is what's wrong. She gave me head last night and I ate her out this morning." Dylan started clapping and I looked at him with anger.

"Dude, you should be happy. That's what you wanted, right?"

"No. I wanted to fuck the shit outta her until she couldn't walk. This bitch said she doesn't wanna anything sexual because she's looking for fucking love. LOVE GOD DAMMIT!"

"Why are you mad? You could fuck any of these other bitches. Or call up Cristella, Cristina, Kristen, whatever the fuck her name is." Emilio was raising his voice at me.

"Yeah dude, call up that old fuck buddy of yours and make Ashley jealous. Then she'll want to give herself to you." Dylan made a good point, but if I did that, Ashley would hate me.

"I can't do that." They looked at each other then looked at me as if I were crazy. "I mean, I haven't been inside of a pussy in a while. But, I'm really trying to make a good impression on Ashley, so that she'll let me have her."

"Once you start fucking her, you should let us get some of that ass too. It's real nice, and she's beautiful. She's literally a pornstar but better." Emilio said as if this were funny.

"NO." I stood up angrily. The look on both of their faces were of fear. "She's mine and only mine, you got that?" They both nodded. I pointed to the door and they both got the message. I sat back down in my chair and scanned my office. Shit was everywhere.

"SAM." I yelled from my office chair. In a matter of seconds, Sam was inside of my office. He looked scared, what a scrawny little thing he was. But he was very violent, I've seen him kill 3 people, a bullet in each head and shake it off as if it were nothing.

"Yes?" He scanned my office.

"I need new office equipment. Make sure everything that's broken or not in its place is thrown out and replaced with something newer and better." He quickly nodded his head and turned around.

I was eyeing my phone on my desk. It was just laying there silent and unbothered until someone decided to call it. I looked at the caller ID and wondered if I should actually answer it. It was Cristina. To hell with it.

"Hello?"

"Hey babe, I was wondering if I could come over and spend the week with you."

"A whole week? Why?"

"I've missed you, silly." She giggled. "Also because that charity gala is in 6 days, and since we are both going... I was wondering if we could go together!" Shit, I forgot about that. She sounded a little too excited. She just loves when people see us together, because it makes her feel as if we are dating. But, we aren't.

"Yeah, sure come over." I rolled my eyes. I really didn't want her to spend 6 days with me at my place. "Why can't you stay at a hotel?"

"Why don't you want me at your place?" She asked. I groaned, not wanting to tell her that there was another female at my pent.

"Fine, come over. When will you be there?"

"Give me an hour." Dammit. That bitch was already on her way to my place.

"Bye." I hung up abruptly and grabbed my stuff and left. I told Sam that I was going home.

―――――――――――――――

(A/N) I hope all you horny little people liked this chapter. Anyway, on to the next chapter. I've been really in the mood to write, so that's why a few chapters will be published.

Peace from the Middle East.

(16) And Who's This?

Ashley's POV

I was sitting in the living room watching TV until Kyle walked through the door. He looked at me and then looked away and headed for his bedroom. When he came back, he was dressed more casual and looked a little mad.

"Go to your room." He commanded. He stood close to me and pointed to my room.

"Why?" I'm confused as to what got him in a bad mood. I mean, when we left the restaurant he was a lot more mad than he was when he got there.

"I SAID GO TO YOUR ROOM." He yelled at me. I jumped up and scurried to my room and locked the door. Luckily my iPod was on the nightstand. I could watch Netflix on it, listen to music or play games. The only thing I couldn't do was send messages. He deleted the messages and email app. And to buy things from the App Store, I would need the password that only he knows.

****

After 2 hours of watching Netflix, I became pretty tired. I plugged my iPod to the charger and just snuggled into blankets. Now that it was quiet in my room, I could hear a female talking. And I would hear Kyle talk back to her.

Wow. He really told me to stay in my room because he was going to hookup with someone. I mean, I didn't want to see him hookup with anyone. That's nasty. Welp, I guess the only thing to do to prevent me from hearing any sexual sounds was to go to sleep. That's exactly what I did. I woke up at around 7pm.

Oops. I was supposed to make dinner. I put some pajamas on, so that I wouldn't mess up my regular clothes. I hope that woman isn't here anymore, and they both got what they needed out of their system. I opened my bedroom door and peeked out, to make sure the coast was clear. When everything seemed fine, I walked out of my room and into the kitchen to start cooking. I started going through the fridge to see what I would make. I figured that I would make some fried chicken tenders, sweet potatoes and corn. I pulled all the ingredients out and I heard talking. I chose to ignore it, which was a bad mistake.

I saw Kyle in just boxers and the girl was in lingerie. I must've looked like a deer caught in headlights. I was so scared, I wasn't able to speak. Kyle looked pissed off and the woman looked pissed but also shocked. She didn't cover her body when she saw me, instead she crossed her arms over her chest.

"Kyle call the cops. Some..." she eyed me down. "ugly person broke into our home." She sounded stuck up. I was offended that she called me ugly. Like, I know I'm not super skinny, or tall or have the most symmetrical face, but I'm not ugly. On top of that, she said that this was her house. I thought only Kyle lived here. It was hard to tell because there weren't any pictures or anything that could've signaled that a woman lived here.

"She didn't break in." He looked at me angrily. "She's a friend and she's staying with me for a while." He looked back at the scandalously dressed woman. She pouted angrily, like a child who didn't get candy from the candy store.

"Umm. Who's this?" I asked Kyle. I said it with a slight attitude. I looked at this Barbie-looking woman.

"I'm Cristina, Kyle's girlfriend." She wrapped her arms around him possessively.

"Anyway, I was gonna cook dinner if you still want it." I started preparing to cook once again.

His next words shocked me and made me slightly angry. "Yeah. As much as I ate her out, I'm still a little hungry." He gave me an evil smirk and she looked confused. I gulped and continued cooking.

As I cooked, I would occasionally glance at the two on the couch. They were all over each other. Kissing, touching, and she was grinding in his lap. It made me sick.

•*•*•*•*•*•*•*•*•*•*•*•*•*•*•*•*•*•*•

Kyle's POV

As we ate dinner, I carefully watched Ashley. I wanted to see if she was jealous. She looked more pissed off than anything else. Cristina sat next to me and couldn't keep her hands or feet off of me. Whenever I would tell her to stop, she would just bat her eyelashes and act all innocent.

"What's your name?" Cristina asked Ashley. I knew Cristina all too well, and I knew that she was going to try to get in Ashley's last nerve, then blame everything on Ashley.

"Ashley." She said coldly.

"Why don't you stay at your place?" Ashley looked up at me, then smiled wickedly. I knew she wasn't going to tell Cristina that she was kidnapped, but Ashley is unpredictable.

"Hmm." Ashley thought about it. I don't know what she's up to, but it's not good. "Why don't you stay at yours?" The smile on Ashley's face disappeared after saying that.

"Lose the attitude before you lose a place to stay. And technically, this is my place. I come here often and I know where everything is." She rudely said to Ashley. I felt bad for Ashley. She walked right into a trap. Hopefully Cristina doesn't try to hurt Ashley.

"Ashley clean up and go to your room." I got up from the table and walked to my room.

****

The next 2 days were living hell. Cristina wanted to spend all the time in the world with me, while I just wanted to go to work. We went shopping for dresses and tuxes. We went regular clothes shopping. In return, we all know what I got. Sex. It was good sex, I guess. Sometimes I would fantasize that I was fucking Ashley and that would make me cum quicker.

I am at the mall with Cristina, and we were currently looking for shoes, jewelry, accessories and etc. I am so bored. I tried making up excuses, but to no avail. Cristina would throw a temper tantrum saying that 'I don't love her' or 'all I wanna do is spend time with you and you don't want to spend time with me, do you even like me?' People walking passed us would look at us and shake their heads at me. I truly didn't care, so I don't know what made me want to stay.

•••

Chase's POV

I was in front of Kyle's door, talking to the guards. I asked them if Kyle was here and they said no, I asked them if Ashley was here and they said yes. They opened the door for me and I walked in. Ashley was there sitting on the couch. She turned around abruptly and got up excitedly. I placed the food on the counter and she jumped into my arms in a hug.

"Hey Chase!" I put her down.

"Hey beautiful! I got you some food, I wasn't too sure if you ate or not."

She looked inside the bag and looked confused. "How do you know what I like from Chick-fil-a?" She went to go sit on the couch.

"Last time I was here, we asked each other questions. You told me what you liked."

"Oh yeah!" She started laughing. "Did you get anything to drink?" I shook my head.

"I thought you would have something here to drink." I walked to the fridge and opened it up. I took out a Sprite and a Rootbeer. "See? Drinks." I joined her on the couch to eat and watch Netflix.

"Why'd you come over? Not that I don't want you here." She asked out of the blue.

"You want me here?" I acted honored. She smiled at me then giggled. She was adorable, hot, kind, funny. What else could you ask for in a girl? "Well I wanted to see you again, and hang out."

"Well if you came here to hang out, we're gonna do it the Ashley way. I'll be right back." She got up swiftly and ran to her room. On her way back out, I realized she had a speaker and an iPod.

"Can I see your iPod for a second?" She nodded and handed it over to me. I unlocked it and went to her contacts. It asked for a passcode to unlock the feature, and knowing Kyle, I knew what it would be. His mother's name. I put my FaceTime information into her iPod and FaceTimed my phone to get her info. She looked at me curiously.

"Now we can talk whenever we want to." I smiled at her and handed her back her iPod.

"Coolio." She started to connect the speaker and her iPod and played some music. The first song that played was Wannabe by the Spice Girls. She started singing and dancing around me. She grabbed my hand and pulled me off the couch so I could join her. I knew some of the words, so I sung along with her. We danced around the living room, the dinning room, the kitchen. We stood on top of the counter and on tables.

The next song was Often by The Weeknd and she froze. I started laughing, and decided to sing the song before she would change it. She jumped off the couch and was about to change the song until I grabbed her and sung the song to her.

"She asked me if I do this everyday, I said often." We rocked side to side while she laughed. "I asked her how many times she rode the wave-"

"Not so often." She said at the right time. I let go of her and she started to grind on me. The way she was grinding on me felt like fucking heaven. If she hasn't rode the wave in a while, she's about to soon. I danced along with her. My dick started to get hard, I have no doubt that she felt it. She turned back around and started laughing.

"You sure you don't ride the wave often?" She chuckled and nodded her head. She turned back around and started doing it again and sung at the same time. Honestly, I'm thinking about asking this girl to be mine. I love the way her ass feels on me. I placed my hands on her hips and kept going along with her movements.

The front door of the penthouse opened. And there stood a shocked Cristina and an angry Kyle. I smiled and Ashley stood up quickly. I looked at Ashley's face and could see that she was embarrassed and blushing. She rushed to turn off the music.

"Leave you skank. And Chase, you can leave with her." Cristina shrieked at us. My jaw clenched. I didn't appreciate Cristina who's a whore, calling Ashley who's an angel, a skank.

"Dude get this bitch before I put her in her fucking place." I yelled at him. I was pissed.

"Who the fuck are you yelling at." Kyle walked up to me as if he wanted to fight. I was ready for it. If he wasn't going to control that bitch, Cristina, then he's a bitch. Like how the fuck are you going to let Cristina treat Ashley like that. He kidnapped Ashley, he should at least be on Ashley's side.

"I'm yelling at you, you stupid bitch." I cracked my knuckles. "How you gonna let a bitch treat Ashley like that. Huh? Punk." Kyle's jaw clenched and he was obviously infuriated. He swung and I dodged it and I landed one on his jaw. He stumbled back and grabbed his jaw. He walked up to me as if he was about to punch me. Ashley ran in between us and tried to push us apart. But it was too late. Kyle had already started to swing at me, but instead of hitting me in the side, he hit Ashley on the jaw. Ashley fell onto the ground and was gripping her jaw. She was crying and sitting there, just looking at Kyle.

Cristina giggled. I looked at her with my death glare and she wiped that smile off her face.

Kyle looked scared. He dropped to his knees to try to calm Ashley down. Ashley scooted away from him, as if his touch would burn her.

"Oh my God. I'm so sorry Ashley." He tried to grab her wrist, but I moved in front of Ashley to prevent that.

"Get the fuck away from her, you hurt her. Whose to say it wasn't on purpose?" I turned around and picked Ashley up from the ground. I carried her to her room and placed her in her bed. I went to her bathroom and got some tissue for her, so that she could wipe her tears away. I then walked into the kitchen to get her a bag full of ice, water and a pain reliever. I glanced at Kyle who looked stressed and sorrowful. That's what he gets, he should feel bad. He hurt Ashley. As I walked into the room I heard Cristina say something so unforgettable.

"Babe, stop beating yourself up. She's probably faking it for attention. You probably didn't even hit her that hard." I was even more pissed. I debated whether I should curse this bitch out now or I should tend to Ashley. Since I like Ashley a lot more than Cristina, I chose to tend to Ashley. I walked inside of Ashley's room and listened to Kyle yell at Cristina. Finally, that punk needed to put Cristina in her place.

I sat next to Ashley and handed her the ice to put on her jaw. I took out an Advil and handed her the glass of water to take. After she took it, she put the ice back on her jaw.

"Let me see it." She turned her head the the side a little, so that I was able to look at where she got punched. There was a nice size bruise. "Does it feel broken?" I was worried, what if it was broken. Then she wouldn't be able to give me blowjobs for a while, while we date.

She chuckled, "No it doesn't feel broken. But it hurts like a bitch." I laughed. "What's going on in there?" My demeanor changed. I don't like Kyle for what he did to Ashley.

"Cristina said something rude. And that punk finally put that bitch in her place. I don't know how he can stand her." She laughed and I was glad. I loved her smile.

"She's annoying and a snarky little thing. But, he does need sex, and I'm not willing to do the nasty with him." I laughed and so did she. We stared at each other for a while, then things got kinda awkward.

"This might not be the right time to ask you this. But, this weekend is the charity gala... I wanted you to be my plus one. If you don't mind." I said. I was a little nervous. What if she says no, and I've been reading our situation the wrong way.

"Sure. I've never been to a charity gala before. I don't think I have anything appropriate for one either. So we'd need to go shopping." She smiled at me. It was like time froze and all the was there was her and I. "Wait. What about my jaw? Pretty sure there's a bruise there."

"If you don't have makeup, then we can buy some, so that you could cover it up."

I gave her a hug and a quick kiss on the cheek. She blushed and I left. I can't believe I like the girl that Kyle wants. I saw Kyle still stressing over what he did to Ashley. I guess he saw me out the corner of his eyes because he stood up and walked over to me.

"How is she? Is she ok? Does she want to talk to me or anything?" He asked worriedly.

"Why would she want to talk to the person that hit her? But yeah, she's fine. And guess who's coming with me to the gala." I smiled at him and left his house. As I stood in the elevator, I thought of Ashley. What it would be like to fuck her, make love to her, kiss her. And so on. The next thing I have to do is take her shopping. Probably tomorrow, and if I need to spend all my money on her, then so be it.

(A/N) honestly I need to find a guy like Kyle, because Kyle is honestly just so... nice. Anyways... I hope you guys have a wonderful thanksgiving (for all those who are celebrating). If you're not celebrating than have a happy November 24th.

(17) Gala Shopping

Ashley's POV

I was outside of CVS waiting in Chase's car. He was currently getting foundation, concealer, setting powder, brushes and a beauty blender. I needed to cover my bruise before going shopping. He came outside with 2 plastic bags, when he got into the car he handed the bags to me.

"Here ya go, beautiful." He smiled at me and I returned the favor. I looked inside the bags and found that he bought a lot more than we needed.

"We don't need all of this ya know." I looked up at him.

"Really? This teen girl in there told me what to buy. She lied to me." He faked a betrayed face and then started laughing. I started to apply the makeup with the little knowledge I have of makeup. I'm pretty sure foundation goes first, then concealer. I placed the foundation on my face and blended it using the beauty blender. The bruise wasn't fully covered, so I guess I'm going to have to use concealer. I applied that and blended it in. The bruise looked pretty covered and I didn't have a cake face. I set my face with setting powder, and I was finished. I looked in the bag to see what else was in there. There was bronzer, mascara, highlight, makeup remover wipes and eye liner. Plus, two shades of red lipstick. I decided to go all out and put everything on my face. He started to drive to the mall, while I 'beat' my face.

Once we arrived, I had finally finished. Chase looked at me and looked surprised.

"What? Is it bad?" I asked nervously.

He shook his head no. "No, I didn't know that you were so good makeup." I was shocked that he thought it looked nice. I mean, I thought it looked nice. But who knows?

"Oh, thank you." He got out the car and I did the same. We walked to the mall and we made small talk. Out of nowhere, he decided to hold my hand. It wasn't weird, so I didn't pull away. I looked up at him and he acted if this was a regular thing. One thing I noticed as he held my hand, is that it doesn't feel the same as when Kyle held my hand. Yeah, it's a bad thing that I'm comparing the two, but it's the truth.

Inside the mall, we visited a few stores. I loved going to the mall so much. I love spending money on clothes, shoes and food. We visited Victoria's Secret/Pink. Chase would pick up a bra or underwear that he thought was cute and ask me if I wanted it. Sometimes, he would put the bra on his chest and ask me if it suited him. We laughed and kept shopping.

"Maybe we should come back here after you get your dress, so we know what kind of bra and underwear you need." Chase suggested as we looked at underwear.

"Okay." I said and walked towards him, so we could walk out the store together. He instantly reached for my hand when we were close enough. We went to a few dress stores, looking for a dress appropriate for the gala. I tried a lot of them on and modeled for Chase. I would act like a fool. Sometimes I would dance or sing. Sometimes I even pretended to be on a runway. He and I were having such a fun time. We left the dressing room and I saw a beautiful dress on a mannequin. It was a blush color and it was gorgeous. I asked an employee to find it in my size. She looked me up and down and then walked away. Chase and I sat on the closest seat and just talked.

"So what are these galas like? What am I supposed to expect." I asked him.

He chuckled. "Well. They're full of people rich and people in the middle-class. There's classic music and jazz playing most of the time. There are tables to eat our 4 course meal. Then the auction begins. Though the gala we're going to is going to have a raffle, bake sale, auction and talent show. So be ready to be amazed or bored to death." The sales woman came back with my dress and lead me to the dressing rooms. I tried the dress on, which was sort of a struggle. It didn't have a zipper or holes that actually told you if your arm or head was supposed to go through it. Once I had it on, I looked in the mirror.

Damn. This dress is beautiful. I looked at it from the sides and admired it on my body. I walked out the dressing room and showed Chase the dress while it was on me. He was definitely shocked.

"You're gorgeous." Was the only thing he said. I blushed and felt special. "We are buying this dress. How much is it?" I shrugged my shoulders and walked closer towards him so he could find the tag. He found it and looked at it.

"So how much is it?" I asked him.

"Don't worry about it." He gave me a reassuring smile and I walked back into the dressing room to put my regular clothes on. We purchased the dress and it was $1026.99. I was surprised he even bought it. We walked around the mall some more and found a jewelry store. He told me to pick some jewelry out to wear with my dress. I found a slim diamond choker and it was just beautiful.

"If you like chokers, I'll get you one that say's 'Daddy's ' or 'baby girl'." He winked at me and smiled.

"Hmm. I wonder who I would wear that for. Because I don't call anyone daddy." He smirked. An idea popped into my head. I should tease him again. It's really funny, because he thinks I'm being serious with him. We purchased the choker and left the store. We were in our way to a shoe store, but I was really hungry. My stomach kept growling and I just wanted something to eat.

I tugged on Chase's hand and he looked down at me. "I'm hungry." I smiled mischievously. "Daddy." His eyes went wide and he gulped.

"Uh. Yeah. Ok. Um. What do you want to eat?" I can tell I surprised him because he was acting so weird. I bit my lip and thought about it.

"Can we get Chipotle?"

"Anything for you baby girl." Now I was the one who was shocked. I was surprised he would call me something like that. I mean, he usually just calls me beautiful, and baby girl is on a whole different level. We walked up to the directory and located Chipotle. Once we found it, we started our journey. As we walked, we talked about what he does for a living. He told me that he's in an organization that's really hard to get into. He asked me what I wanted to do when I get older and I told him. I told him that I wanted to go to Med School to get my PhD. I really wanted to become a reconstruction surgeon. I wanted to help people feel better about themselves. And because I'm funny, they'll feel better inside and out. Once we arrived at Chipotle, I ordered my bowl with white rice, black beans, chicken, corn, and cheese. With guacamole and sour cream on the side.

With no doubt, I knew that Chase was going to try and remember my order. He ordered his burrito after me.

There was no surprise when he finished that burrito all by himself. I had seen Taylor eat a burrito all by herself in sophomore year of high school. We left Chipotle and went to a few shoe stores. I found the perfect pair of lace up heels to go with my dress. We had to go back to Victoria's Secret to get a bra and underwear to wear underneath my dress. Once we walked in, Chase said something.

"I don't think you should wear a bra." Chase said as he looked at a few of them. I looked at him quickly and furrowed my eyebrows.

"Why not?" I asked in curiosity. I kept looking for a bra.

"The strapless ones will be seen in the back and regular ones could be seen everywhere. So you shouldn't wear a bra." I understood what he's saying, but I don't know if I'm ready to go to my first gala braless, or being in front of a lot of people braless.

"I don't know. What if it gets cold? Or what if people start looking at my chest?" I asked him. I was starting to think that going braless was the best answer.

"If it gets cold, then I'll warm you up. And if anyone looks at your chest, tell me and I'll make them regret it." I laughed.

"Fine. Since we aren't getting anything from here, we can leave." I walked towards the front of the store. He grabbed my hand and pulled me back.

"You still need underwear." He said with a smile.

"I have underwear already."

"Did I pick it out?" He raised his eyebrows. "Didn't think so, now come on baby girl. Let's get you a thong." He's still playing this game? I need to step it up.

He walked over the where the most thongs were located and looked for a lace one. I didn't help him, because I already had underwear at Kyle's house. I don't need more.

"Found it." He held up a lace baby pink thong. It was a really pretty thong I have to admit. We bought it. The lady at the cash register kept trying to flirt with Chase, but he was having no part of it. I guess he sensed what the woman was doing because he pulled me closer towards him and told me I looked beautiful. The woman at the register rolled her eyes and proceeded to do her job. We left the store and felt content. After 4 hours of shopping, we were finally done. We walked back to Chase's car, while talking about the gala. Once we got to the car, we put everything in the trunk. I was walking to my side of the car when Chase pushed me against the car. I was about to scream until he put his hands on either side of my face and leaned in. I closed my eyes and waited for his lips to touch mine. He kissed me with so much fiery and lust. He lifted me up and I wrapped my legs around him and my arms around his neck. As we kissed, it felt like we were the only people in the world. It was just him and I. His mouth was an expert and his lips were soft. We kissed until someone snapped us out of it.

"Excuse me, I need to get into my car. So if you don't mind taking that somewhere else." We broke the kiss. Chase was still holding me, so he moved so the man could get into his car. Chase was staring into my eyes. And I stared back into his brown ones. We were lost in each other. He had made me wet and I had no doubt that I had made him hard. He put me down and I was blushing like crazy. I walked back to the passenger seat and got into the car. I can't believe that just happened. I just kissed Chase. Where is all of this freakiness coming from? Because I was certainly not like this before. We drove in silence, occasionally he would look over at me and smile. We stopped at a red light and he put his hand on my thigh. The fact that I was turned on earlier and now that he's touching my bare leg, I don't know what might happen.

"Are you ok?" He asked sincerely. I nodded. Afraid to talk. Afraid that my voice might sound squeaky or something.

"If you're mad that I kissed you, then I'm sorry. I just.." he sighed. I looked over to him and the light turned green. "I guess I just like you a lot." What? He what now? Umm... this is definitely not ok. I barely know this dude.

He drove me to Kyle's penthouse and helped me carry everything upstairs. In the elevator I put the bags down. I turned to him.

"I'm not upset that you kissed me. It was a really.... interesting kiss." I smiled at him hoping to relieve the anxiety that was building inside of him.

"Good. I'm hoping to do it sometime soon, baby girl." He winked at me and we laughed. The doors of the elevator opened and we walked to Kyle's house and into my room. We put everything away and hung the dress up so it wouldn't wrinkle.

We walked out of my room and I noticed that Kyle and Cristina were sitting in on the couch. Chase sat in the armchair and I wanted to win this game. So guess what I did. I sat in his lap. Sure, he was shocked and so was Kyle who was watching the two of us. I wiggled my butt around, so that I could get comfortable. I giggled. Chase laid his hands on top of my thighs and we sat there. Kyle kept looking over at us, I don't know why. He shouldn't be jealous. He has Cristina, right? According to her they're dating, so he shouldn't have a problem with me doing this. Yet, he looked angry.

"If I call him daddy. He know he gettin' in the panties. So daddy, daddy, daddy, daddy, daddy, daddy, daddy!" I blurted out. Everyone stared at me but I had a huge grin on my face.

"What was that Ashley?" Kyle seethed.

"It's this thing I saw on Instagram. I thought it was catchy." Kyle didn't look any more impressed.

"Baby girl, I don't think you should tell certain people that." Chase said to me. Kyle heard what Chase said and got angrier.

"Hey daddy." Cristina seductively said to Kyle. Kyle looked at her then stormed to his room. He slammed the door shut. We sat there shocked. Cristina looked as if she didn't know to go after him or sit there and act like nothing happened. We all sat there, continuing to watch Keeping Up With The Kardashians, which must've been Cristina's favorite TV show.

We sat there for another hour watching various TV shows. Kyle came out of his room and saw that I was still sitting in Chase's lap. He just stared at me, I don't know why, but it's weird. Chase saw what was happening.

"Baby girl could you get off my lap please?" I got off of Chase's lap and stood up in front of him. Chase stood up and stretched. We walked to the door together and Kyle just watched us. Chase gave me a hug. Then out of nowhere he kissed me. It wasn't a quick peck, but it wasn't like our make out session earlier. I stood on my tippy toes. After a little bit, we parted and he said goodbye.

I walked back to my room, but Kyle stood in front of the door. I crossed my arms and looked at him angrily.

"What do you want?" I asked him.

"We need to talk." He turned around and walked into my room. He sat on my bed, and I closed my bedroom door. Not knowing what to expect. I stood up in front of him, waiting for him to start speaking.

"So, he's your boyfriend?" He asked.

"That's none of your concern."

"You live here, and he keeps coming here. So it is my concern. So answer my question Ashley." He raised his voice a little.

"No, he's not my boyfriend. Why does that matter to you? You have Cristina and I have Chase."

"So, he's your fuck buddy? I thought you had to be in love. What happened to that?"

"He's not my fuck buddy. He's my friend. A friend that takes care of people and doesn't punch people in the face." I directed that one at him.

"So you kiss your friends like that? You grind on their dicks? And what happened was an accident. We both know I didn't mean to hit you."

"It doesn't matter what I do to my friends. And how would I know if that was an accident. You seemed pretty angry after I told you we couldn't do that stuff to each other. You seemed mad when Chase called you out on your shit. So whose to know if you punched me on purpose or not. Why do you care so much, huh? You act like you don't go around doing nasty shit with people all the time. You make me feel as if I'm a slut for having fun with one guy. Stop worrying about me and worry about yourself." He kept quiet and listened to my rant. I was actually yelling at his face. I was just so upset with him. Surprisingly I wasn't crying while yelling at him. Whenever I'm really mad or frustrated, tears pour out like a waterfall and I don't know how to make them stop.

He grabbed my wrist and pulled me towards him. He put his hands on either side of my hips and forced me to sit on his lap while facing him. Even in these circumstances, I still felt a tingle whenever Kyle touched me.

"Let go of me Kyle." I tried pushing myself off of him, but his grip didn't give.

"Tell me honestly. Does it feel the same when you touch him versus when we are touching? Does he make you feel this good?" I was confused as to what he meant by this good. Soon I found out.

Kyle grabbed both sides of my face and kissed me. His lips felt heavenly compared to Chase's lips. It was like lightning had struck me, but it felt like a good lightning. I was shocked at first; his talented mouth working over my inexperienced one. Soon I gave in, I kissed him back and it was magical. His hands were running up and down my back. While one of my hands were on the back of his neck and the other one in his hair. He kiss was fiery, lustful and nice. He leaned back on the bed and allowed me to be on top. His hands roamed onto my ass he grabbed it. I let out a small moan and I felt him smile. I sat up and realized I was sitting on his crotch. I quickly got up and he just smiled as if it was funny.

"How was that?" He asked me. My face felt heated and I was extremely wet. I could feel my panties clinging to me. I definitely felt something more when kissing Kyle than I did with Chase. But I have no idea why. I would rather date Chase, he's just a nicer guy.

"It was..." I was trying to think of a good word for what I felt.

"Don't lie to me Ashley." He was now standing in front of me, with his hand on the side of my face with the bruise. His other hand was on my side, pulling my body into his. My hands rested on his chest and we stared into each other's eyes.

"It felt nice. I guess." I didn't want to say it felt wonderful or magical. I didn't want to say I liked the kiss, because I knew he wasn't looking for a relationship. He was looking for someone to help satisfy his needs and I was not that person.

He gave me a peck on my lips and walked out of my room. My stomach was left doing somersaults and it was making me feel... I don't know. It's like going on a high roller coaster with a big drop. And the feeling you get while it goes down, is how I'm feeling currently. It wasn't a bad feeling, just a weird one.

Now what was I supposed to do? I kissed two hot guys in one day. Looks like I'm going to have to chose one.

(A/N) this chapter was longer than I attended it to be. But I'm happy with how it turned out. Honestly, I need someone that won't mind spending their money and time on me and treating me like the princess I am.

Don't forget to vote and comment. Keep reading and hasta luego.

(18) The Gala

Ashley's POV

Ever since Thursday, I've been trying to avoid Kyle at all costs. I would cook dinner and while I was cooking, he would come watch me cook. He was always shirtless, probably having just finishing pleasing Cristina or vice versa. He would try to talk to me, but I would give him a short, quick answer or I would nod or shake my head. This happened for 2 days with most meals, unless he wasn't home. The rest of the day, would be spent inside my room texting or FaceTiming Chase. It was really fun because he was really funny. We continued playing our little game, to see who would fall first. I definitely am not easy to be won, but I liked him, I just wouldn't let him notice.

It was finally Saturday and I was extremely excited for my first gala. The only thing I wasn't happy about was that I had started my period last night and I wouldn't be able to wear the thong that Chase had chosen. I still was going to wear some cute underwear. Chase picked me up around 7 this morning, in order for me to go get everything done. The first thing that I did was get my nails done. I got them painted white, while my ring finger was painted a shimmery gold. After I got my nails done, we went out for breakfast at IHOP. I got a waffle with bacon and Chase got French toast, eggs, bacon, and fruit. And occasionally he would steal a piece of my waffle and I would steal a piece of French toast as revenge. It was around 9:45 am, and I went to the hair salon to get my hair washed and styled. Chase left me there, and went to the barber shop. About an hour later, he came back and saw that I wasn't done. They were curling my hair and it was going to be beautiful. We talked and laughed a lot while I sat in the chair getting my hair done.

"I like your hair." I said with a smile.

"Thank you!"

"It reminds me of all the fuckboys that went to my high school. They all had the same haircut." I started laughing and he did a fake angry face, then joined in on the laughter.

The hair stylist left rollers in my hair, so that whenever I'm ready I could take them out and my hair would still be curled. Chase paid them and we left.

"Baby girl. That wasn't nice." Chase didn't unlock the car, so I was just standing there. He walked in front of me and put a hand on either side of my body, caging me in. My eyes went wide and I blushed.

"What are you talking about daddy?" I said with a smirk. He groaned and his face started moving towards mine quickly. Soon his lips were on mine and we were kissing. His hands moved to my hips, pulling me closer to him. My arms wrapped around his neck. While we were kissing, I remembered what happened last night. Kyle kissed me. Kyle's kiss was amazing and compared to this one... Kyle's was greater. Before I could separate myself. Out the corner of my eye, I saw a teen girl with her phone out, probably taking a picture of us. I started laughing and we stopped kissing. The girl looked scared that she got caught and quickly walked away.

"What's so funny?"

"This girl took a picture of us. A teenage girl." He chuckled. He unlocked the car and opened the door for me. He drove me back to Kyle's place and told me that he was going to pick me up at 7:45 pm. The gala started at 8pm, and he told me it would be a 30 minute drive. He just didn't want to get there on time. While we drove he told me how to make a bruise disappear or at least the color. He told me either leave a banana peel on it for 10-30 minutes or a cloth with vinegar on it. I was definitely going to use the banana method first because I'm not too fond of the smell of vinegar. Once we pulled up to the building, I got out, thinking that Chase was just dropping me off. Instead, he got out the car too. As he walked to the door of the building, I ran and jumped on his back. Thankful for his fast reflexes, or else I would've busted my butt when I fell. He carried me to the elevator and into Kyle's house. Once we got in, he put me down. Kyle was on the couch watching Netflix while Cristina was giving him a nice blow down under. Kyle looked shocked that I was back, and then shocked turned to anger. There goes that jealousy again.

"Ew." I said and I grabbed Chase's hand and walked into my room. Chase laughed at my response to what I just saw.

"I'll be right back baby girl." He walked out of my room. About 5 minutes later he walked back in with a bowl and a banana peel. He handed me the banana peel to put on my face and he kept the bowl with banana to himself. I removed the makeup that I had to put on to cover the bruise. I laid down in bed and put the banana peel on my face. Chase ate the banana and bid me farewell.

Once he left I decided to take a nap and wake up around 2 and eat lunch.

****

It's 6:45 and I have an hour before Chase gets here to pick me up for the gala. I went to the bathroom to brush my teeth and take a shower, and noticed that the bruise had went away. I played some music on the speaker as I got ready for the gala. At around 7:30, Chase sent me a text saying that he was on his way. I already had my dress on, and took the rollers out. I had put the choker on and my heels and right now, I am dancing and singing around my room. I wanted to look and smell good, so I had added some mascara, eyeliner and a matte lipstick. I also put on some perfume. I lost track of time because I heard a banging on my door and I paused the music. I opened the door to see a handsomely dressed Chase with a bow tie that matched the color of my dress.

"Wow! You look... gorgeous." He sounded astonished. I blushed and grabbed his hand.

"You clean up well yourself."

"Well, I always look this good."

"Are you saying I don't look good all the time?" I faked a pout.

"Baby girl, you always look beautiful." He kissed my forehead and pulled me out of my room.

"Hold on I need to get my stuff." I went back into my room and grabbed the lipstick, my iPod, and a pad just incase. "Hey can you hold this?" I gave everything to Chase and he looked at the pad with wide eyes.

"You're on your period?"

"Yup. Why is that such a shocker? Most girls get it."

He pretended to act sad. "So you're not wearing the thong I got you?" I shook my head no. "Okay, when you get off of your period, could you possibly model it for me?" I laughed.

"I don't know. We'll see." He stood there dumbstruck.

I walked into the living room, right when Kyle walked into the living room. Kyle looked breathtaking. I mean I've seen him in suits before, but something about him is just more alluring. He looked at me with wide eyes. He smiled then winked. Cristina came out after he did, in a skin tight, red lace dress. She looked even more like a Barbie. Her makeup was heavier and she wore a bright red lipstick. Kyle walked up to me and gave me a hug. I hugged him back, and he smelt so manly. His hug was comforting and I felt protected in his arms, which is weird to say.

"You look stunning." He whispered in my ear. I was still shorter than him, even in 5-inch heels. We broke apart after some time, and I caught Cristina giving me a cold glare. I turned around to Chase who was doing the same to Kyle. Chase grabbed my hand and pulled me into his body swiftly. I let out a yelp, and soon after, his lips were on mine. I kissed Chase back, but it felt weird to do that when I had kissed Kyle just a few nights ago. I felt Chase's hand travel to my butt, and give it a squeeze. When we broke the kiss, he wasn't as mad anymore.

"Kyle, I'll see you at the gala." Chase said. Chase grabbed ahold of my hand and started walking towards the door.

"Actually. I'm having a limo pick all of us up. It should be here soon." Chase turned around and gave Kyle a grim look. Chase sighed and I looked up at him, I wanted to know if he was ok. I could see his jaw clenching and unclenching. I lifted his hand towards my face and kissed his hand. It shocked him well enough. He looked down at me kind of confused. I gave him a reassuring smile, letting him know everything was okay. We walked over to the couch and Chase sat down first. Once he sat down, he grabbed onto my waist and pulled me onto his lap. I plopped on his lap, I have no doubt that it hurt when I did that. Cristina got the remote and turned the TV on. Not again, I literally hate this woman. She watches horrible TV shows and she's disrespectful. She turned the channel onto the Bad Girls Club, which was just a show of a whole bunch of girls with beef. I looked over to Kyle, to find him staring at Chase and I.

We watched TV for another 15 minutes, until the limo driver called Kyle, telling him that he was here. We all went to the elevator to go down to the first floor. Kyle kept staring at me, and it was honestly making me so uncomfortable. One of my biggest pet peeves is when someone just stares at me. It's weird, uncomfortable, makes me think that there is something wrong with me or that I can't make a mistake while they stare. All the while, Chase held my hand. When I saw the limo, I was shocked. I mean, I had a limo for my Sweet 16. But this limo was a gold color, like an actual gold color. Shiny and everything. The driver opened the door and Cristina went in first, then me. When I got in, Chase lightly slapped my butt and I yelped. When he got in, he was smiling and winked at me. Chase sat on one side of me and Kyle sat on the other. I don't know why Kyle is sitting so close to me, when his girlfriend is on the other side of the car. She was sitting across from him. The driver got into the car and we were off. I was so excited to go to my first ever gala.

"Let's play some music." Cristina said. You were able to control what music played in the back. She started playing some partying songs. The first song that played was The Fix by Nelly. I used to listen to this song whenever I had a crush on someone. So I sang along, and Chase smiled. After a while, he started singing too. Cristina was giving a Kyle a lap dance. So I gave Chase a lap dance. Chase put his hands on my hips and looked at where our bodies were touching. I could feel his cöck getting harder and he let out a groan. I smiled and wrapped my arms around his neck. The next song was 7/11 by Beyoncé and Cristina and I were dancing around the limo. I had to force myself out of Chase's grip because he didn't want to let go of me. We had a lot of fun dancing and singing in the limo. After a while, the limo stopped and the side door opened. I was the first to get out the limo. There was paparazzi and a big beautiful hotel. The lights that kept flashing blinded me, but I was amazed by how many well-dressed people there were, the paparazzi, the hotel. It was a lot to take in. Chase came out after me and grabbed my hand. As Chase and I walked in, paparazzi kept asking us to stop and take photos of us together. A few times we did stop and pose, when, we did, Chase would pull me close to his body and I loved it. We heard a few people ask if we were dating, but I really don't know what this is. We walked into the building and I looked behind me to see Kyle right behind us, with Cristina next to him. They weren't hold hands or had their arms connected. They just walked side by side.

The hotel or event had put signs everywhere and had ushers to help people get to the room we were all meeting in. There were 2 rooms that the gala was going to be held in. One was the dinning room with a stage. The other room was more like a socializing room, with a stage, bar, dance floor and appetizers. I tugged on Chase's hand and pointed to the appetizers. He smiled, understanding my message and we walked over to get some food. There were a lot of beautiful women and handsome men. I grabbed a small plate and put some appetizers on it. I grabbed mozzarella sticks, garlic bread with turkey slices and shrimp. Chase didn't get anything and I knew he had to be hungry. I mean, I didn't eat before coming, I don't know if he did. We walked around, talking to Chase's acquaintances. I wouldn't listen to what they were saying, I would just smile and act as if I were interested. I followed Chase around while eating my food and smiling at everyone. We regrouped with Kyle and Cristina. I still had a few pieces of shrimp and a mozzarella stick left. Kyle grabbed the mozzarella stick quickly and bit it before I could slap his hand away. I pouted and he gave me a victorious smile. I tapped Chase's shoulder, because he was busy on his phone.

"Daddy." Chase looked at me with a shocked expression. Probably wondering why I wasn't afraid to call him that. "He took my last mozzarella stick and ate it." I whined. Kyle's expression changed to one of annoyance.

"Baby girl I got this." I smiled and giggled. "Dude, can you get Ashley a mozzarella stick?" Chase asked Kyle. Kyle still looked annoyed and slightly angry.

"No, I'm fine. If she kept eating, she would get full, and have no time for the planned meal." Kyle made a good point, but I really wanted that mozzarella stick.

"Good point. Ashley, did you hear what he said?" I nodded my head at Chase and pouted. Just then, some woman walked onto the stage.

"Good evening ladies and gentlemen. Tonight is The Helping Hand for Kids, 15th gala. We have a gala, once every year, in the beginning of summer. So far, we have made over 16 million dollars and we hope to keep raising more and more money. We donated to a lot of charities over the past few years, and helped a lot of kids out. Tonight is going to be a very interesting night. On the left side of this room, we have a table with baked goods on it that children made. In front of the stage we have the table with all the raffle prizes, and tickets. In order to get a ticket, the entry price is set at $50. I know, seems expensive. But you have a chance of winning a one week cruise vacation with one other person, a spa day for 2 and so much more. The talent show will be during dinner, which will be great. And last but not least, the auction will begin right after the talent show. So get ready for an amazing night once again." The lady walked elegantly off the stage and a man walked onto the stage.

"If everyone would please make their way to their designated seat please and thank you. If you don't know where you are sitting, please see one of the ushers on either sides of the dining room."

Chase grabbed my hand, so I wouldn't get lost in the crowd of people migrating to the dining room. He obviously knew where our table was because he didn't ask the ushers. We walked up to the front and sat at our table. Soon after, Kyle walked up to our table without Cristina. "Where's your girlfriend Kyle?" I looked at him and he looked annoyed again.

"She's not my girlfriend first of all. Second, we didn't come as a couple we came separately, just rode in the same limo." I nodded at his response. We sat there awkwardly, no one saying anything to each other. Each table had 8 seats and they were nicely sized spaces, so no one would be too close to someone else. An older man, around 55 or higher came towards the table with two women on his arms. One woman sat right next to Kyle and the other sat on the other side of the man.

"Hello." The man said. He had a deep and rough voice. "I'm Oscar and these two ladies are Diane and Trinity." The woman waved at us with us a smile, but more towards Kyle and Chase.

"Well I'm Kyle Johnson." Kyle spoke aloud.

"I'm Chase McKinley and this is..." chase was going to let me introduce myself.

"I'm Ashley." I smiled. The man across the table was looking at me weirdly and I didn't like it.

Two more people came, it was presumably a couple. You can't tell nowadays. Girls and guys are getting really friendly, even when they're not dating. Take me for an example. I kissed both Kyle and Chase in the same day. I flirt with both of them, more Chase than I do to Kyle. And I'm not dating either one. The man pulled the chair out for the woman, then pushed her in. Wow, a gentleman. He sat down and introduced himself as Aaron and his wife Margaret. The men were all talking about their professions and I was talking to the women about everything. We talked about shopping, movies, money, the gala, and the men we were with. I found out that Margaret got married to Aaron at 21, they had known each other previously from high school. They had been dating and doing the nasty, when Margaret found out she was pregnant. Aaron stayed with her through it all. I didn't like talking to the 2 girls on the other side of the table because they were snooty, and reminded me of Cristina. I wanted to keep talking to Margaret, but Aaron and Chase were sitting in between us. So, we both got up and walked around. We laughed and talked a lot. She reminded me of Taylor, well an older version of Taylor. We saw waiters bring food to the tables, so we decided to head back to our table. When we got back, the food was already there waiting for us. The first thing that was there was a small soup with some bread. I'm not really a fan of soup, so I didn't eat it, but I did eat the bread. That bread was really good too. The next thing they brought out was a salad, they took away the bowls that the soup came in and left. The announcer came back onto the stage and asked everyone how there food was so far. Everyone clapped. The talent show was about to begin, and I'm actually pretty excited. The waiters brought our main dish out. It consisted of a steak, baked potatoes, mixed vegetables, and more bread. I prayed and started cutting into my steak. When I looked up, the curtains on the stage opened up. There was a young girl, probably 11 or 12 standing with a mic. She looked really nervous and I felt bad for her. The music started playing and out of nowhere, this young girl started singing like she belongs in Hollywood. She sung Who Says by Selena Gomez. It was spectacular. After she was done, she got a huge round of applause and the smile on her face was gorgeous. She was so happy that she did well.

****

"Okay ladies and gentlemen. Now that the auction is over, we will be drawing the names for the raffle prize winners." 3 tables were pulled onto the stage with 3 large bowls on each table.

"Our first winner for the couple massage we have, Adam and Eva." People clapped for them as they walked onto the stage to receive their gift card for the massage parlor. "For our second prize, we have a dinner for 2 at Yum by J&M." I looked at Kyle and he looked back at me. He put his hand on my thigh and raised an eyebrow.

"What's your restaurant called again?"

"Yum by J&M." He smiled. "I wanted to get my restaurant out there, so I gave a dinner for two as a prize. Then they can tell people about our wonderful service and food." He kept his hand on my thigh which was comforting and slightly turning me on. He was slowly getting higher and higher up my thigh and I didn't know what to do. I don't think I wanted to do anything about it either. It felt really nice.

"For the one week cruise to the Bahamas, Dominican Republic and Cancún, we have Kyle Johnson and Ashley Rowens." My eyes widened in shock. People started clapping for Kyle and I. I looked towards Kyle, he had stood up and had his hand out for me to grab. I grabbed it and we walked to the stage together to receive our prize. I can't believe Kyle won, and I can't believe that he's taking me. I've never been out of the country before, but I have a passport. The only thing is, it's at my parents' house.

We walked onto the stage and Kyle shook the announcer's hand and smiled towards the crowd. I copied what Kyle did, because if I hadn't, then I would probably look like a fool up here.

****

We were all tired from the gala. I was leaning against Chase and his arm was wrapped around me. I was about to fall asleep when Chase placed a small kiss on my forehead. I smiled a little, and closed my eyes.

"Do you have a passport?" I heard Kyle ask. I opened my eyes and he was looking at me. I nodded my head, too tired to speak.

"Where?"

"My parents' house. I didn't have time to pack before coming to your house." I said to him. Where else would my passport be at. Honestly that was a stupid question.

"Oh yeah. Ok, we are going to have to get you a new one." We we're quiet for the rest of the ride. The last this I remember is falling asleep on Chase.

(A/N) update on my life; I still need a boyfriend that will spoil me, love me and be loyal. Anyways, we all need 2 really hot guys to fight over us, because why not?

See ya next chapter! Don't forget to vote, share, comment, and keep reading because, what do you have to lose?

(19) Cruise

Kyle's POV

Today is the day that we board our cruise ship, and I couldn't be more excited. Ashley had been hanging around Chase a lot more since the gala, and the cruise was a way to get that to change. My goal on the cruise is to get her to do something sexual with me, or something that she has never done before. Maybe she'll do the same for me.

"Are we almost there?" Ashley asked. Chase was driving us to the boarding place to get on the ship. It was around an hour away, but it was worth it.

"About 15 more minutes. Why?" Chase asked her.

"I'm just really bored back here and I really want to go on my VERY FIRST CRUISE!" She squealed in delight.

Chase and I laughed. Once we arrived at the docks, we all got out the car. Chase helped Ashley with her bags, and I carried my own. I brought 2 duffle bags and so did Ashley. We walked to the ship, and gave the man our boarding passes. The man at the desk gave us our room keys and a special bar and club wristband. One of the workers from the boat came and took our luggage on a trolley. I was a little wary of them taking our bags. I had brought my Desert Eagle .50 caliber, one of my most beloved guns.

"You're all good to go folks, enjoy your trip." The man at the desk told us. Chase grabbed Ashley's hand and pulled her close to him. I rolled my eyes, mentally gagging at this scene. Ashley shouldn't be kissing him, she should be kissing me.

"C'mon Ashley." I was really impatient when it came to these two. They gave each other one more kiss and parted ways. Ashley walked up to me and we walked onto the ship side by side.

"Let's go to our room first, then we can explore the ship. Okay?" Ashley nodded and we went to our room. The raffle prize was the biggest sized room on the ship, and the room was literally a small apartment. It had a living room area, a mini kitchen and bar, two bedrooms, a balcony and nice bathrooms and two hot tubs. Our bags were already in the suite when we got there, so all we had to do was bring it into the room that we wanted to sleep in. I decided to relax a little bit and watch some TV.

"Kyle. I'm hungry." Ashley kneeled next to me on the couch. I looked at her. She was wearing a skirt and one of those bralette things that she had me buy. I wonder if she's wearing any underwear. I mean, she should be off her period. The gala was 3 weeks ago, when I saw her hand Chase one of her pads.

"They have a grille a few floors down if you're really hungry." She nodded excitedly. We got up and started heading towards the door. I grabbed my wallet and phone and we left.

"Do you know where it is down stairs?" Ashley asked me.

"We can ask. I saw the map a few times, but never actually memorized it." We walked to the elevators and luckily there was a sign telling people what was on each floor. We went down to the 8th floor and it wasn't that busy.

There were a few people at the grille getting lunch, just like us. Ashley walked in front of me and really quickly. I watched her lovely hips sway in that short skirt of hers. Damn. If only I could grab her ass through her skirt, that would be awesome.

"Table for 2 please." Ashley's voice snapped me out of my trance. The waitress grabbed 2 menus and 2 sets of utensils and lead us to our table. Ashley and I sat at a table for two. The waitress told us that someone would be right with us. Before she left, she gave me a smile and a wink. I would've fucked her on her off hours, or maybe even on her on hours, but Ashley was here. My goal was to get somewhere with Ashley, not these sluts that I'm going to see on this cruise.

"What are you going to eat Ashley?"

"I think I'm going to get the cheeseburger with sweet potato fries. And a Sprite." I nodded.

"I don't know what I'm going to get yet." I kept looking through the menu.

"Later tonight, can we go to the pool?" I looked up at Ashley, to see her staring at me with a smile plastered on her face.

"Possibly. We'll have to see if it's going to be open, and what the weather will be like." She nodded.

"Do you have any games on your phone?"

"No. Where's your iPod?"

"I left it in the room. I don't have any pockets."

A waiter came to our table and took our order. He couldn't get his eyes off of Ashley and it was pissing me off. Every guy wants Ashley, but don't realize that she's mine. It's so frustrating. The waiter walked away with our menus and Ashley and I sat there talking.

"Did you bring any swimsuits for me." I nodded my head. When Ashley went online shopping, we never got her any swimwear just because I didn't think she was going to go swimming anytime soon.

"Yeah, I brought a few bikinis that you might like."

"Ugh. Bikinis give me wedgies. They're not like thongs because they have a thicker material. So it bothers me."

"Who said they weren't thong bikinis?" She looked confused.

"Thong bikinis. You mean the ones that purposely go up your butt crack and show your ass to the whole world? Those ones?"

I shrugged my shoulders. With a mischievous smile I said, "You'll have to wait and see." I winked at her. She giggled and nodded her head. She's adorable. A few minutes passed and our food finally came. It looked and smelled so delicious. I couldn't wait to dig in.

Ashley cut her burger in half and put ketchup on her burger. She bit in and moaned. I love when she moans, I love it even more when I'm the cause of it. Ashley looked at me, somewhat embarrassed for moaning.

"Is it that good?" I asked her. She nodded enthusiastically. I reached over, and grabbed a few fries from her plate. She looked shocked.

"Um. Why did you take my fries, I was gonna eat those?" She looked offended.

"I wanted to try some." I smiled and ate one.

"I've never been so disrespected in my life. No one takes Ashley Rowens' food and gets away with it." She squinted her eyes.

"I paid for it."

"Okay. If you wanted fries you could've asked the waiter. Then you could've paid for those too." I laughed. She really was upset that I took some of her fries.

She bit into her burger angrily while staring dead at me with her adorable death glare.

I ate my steak and potatoes while she finished up her food. I paid the bill and we left the table.

We decided to walk around the ship, to see what was on it.

"When did we leave the docks?" Ashley was looking at the water from the side of the ship.

"I don't know. They did say that we were leaving at 11:45."

We found the pool with the water slide. The clubbing area for adults and kids. The bowling alley. The adult swimming pool which had a bar. We found the spa, more restaurants, a few shops. The dining hall, and some other areas.

Ashley and I plan on going to the adult swimming pool later on.

We got back to the room and it was around 2:35 pm.

"We should watch some movies." Ashley said as she plopped onto the couch.

"Ok. Hopefully they have Netflix, so we can continue watching Orange is the New Black."

I sat down next to her and she leaned against me. Her body is so small, I don't think I'll ever get over it. My arm went around her and I rested my hand on her hip. Luckily they had Orange is the New Black, so we started watching it from where we left off. About 2 episodes later, I realized that

Ashley had dozed off. She was still leaning against me. She's so beautiful when she's sleeping. There was still that thought in the back of my mind, wondering if she was wearing underwear or not. I wasn't gonna check. I did decide to bring her to her room though. I carried her bridal style and laid her on her bed gently. When I did that, her skirt rose up.

Well that answers my question. She's wearing a thong, a lacy one at that. I kept staring at it, as if it would soon disappear. I walked out of her room. I really need to relieve myself. I walked into my room and did just that. I watched porn, but in every video, I imagined Ashley and I fucking.

(A/N) this is a short chapter because the next one is going to be.... interesting. Anyway, I might be moving to a bigger house and I'm soooo excited.

(20) A Drunken Ashley

Kyle's POV

"C'MON ASHLEY!" I am currently standing at the door waiting for Ashley. She just woke up not too long ago, and we were about to go get dinner. I was still in my clothes from earlier, and I believe Ashley was too. But who knows, she might be changing and that's what's taking her so long.

She stumbled out of her room while sticking her foot through her one of her high heels. "Sorry." She walked out of the door and I followed her. In the dining hall, they were having a dinner for all the passengers on the cruise. It started at 6 pm, but Ashley was doing something and it took us a while.

"So are we still going to the pool tonight? I looked at the weather and it's supposed to be 85 degrees."

"Is that what you were doing?"

"Kinda." We were walking really fast to get to the dining hall, since we were already 10 minutes late. I don't know what they're serving, but it better be good.

Once we got to the dining hall, there were a lot of people trying to find tables, and waiters and waitresses trying to help them. I grabbed Ashley's hand and pulled her along with me, so she wouldn't get lost. Her hand was small, but fit nicely in mine. It was also really soft. I mean, I've felt her hand before, but... I don't know. It just feels nice to hold it. Luckily, I found an empty table for 2. I pulled out her chair and she sat in it. I went to the other side of the table and sat down. I sighed loudly. Not thinking that she was going to hear it over all the people in this dining hall. I leaned across the table and told her that I was going to go to the buffet first, and asked her to wait at the table so no one would take it.

They had some really good food. Like ham, steak, pork and fish. I got steak, mash potatoes, rolls, and some collard greens. I went back to sit down at the table, and there were a few guys standing around the table. Ashley was laughing with them, and it pissed me off. This cruise was supposed to be a way for me to get closer to Ashley. I walked over to the table and sat down. The men stared at me, somewhat shocked or frightened. I mean, I would understand their faces. Because when I look pissed off, I look like I can easily kill you on the spot.

"Do you guys need something?" I asked sternly. One of them gulped and they shook their heads. They walked away and Ashley looked confused.

"You scared them off."

"Go get your food." She huffed and then got up abruptly. She stormed off. I didn't feel bad for sending those guys away, for all I know, her and Chase are in a somewhat relationship, which isn't going to last long. And Ashley's mine.

Ashley came back after about 10 or so minutes. She had fried chicken, yams, collard greens, a roll, a small piece of steak and corn. I looked up at her, shocked. I was surprised that someone so little and slim could eat so much. I looked up at her face and could tell that she was still somewhat angry at me.

"Are you gonna eat all of that?" She nodded.

"Why couldn't I talk to those guys?" She wasn't going to drop the subject.

"Don't you have a boyfriend. And plus, all they wanted to do was to get you in bed."

"What the frick is your problem? I already told you that Chase wasn't my boyfriend. We are just friends for the last time. And what makes you and them so different? The first time we met, you tried to get me in bed with you." She had raised her voice. So she wasn't somewhat angry, she was really angry.

"The difference is that my dick is most likely bigger than theirs and I know how to use it. The difference is that I'm irresistible and they're just some fuckboys."

"And your not a fuckboy?" She said sarcastically.

"No."

"If you're able to go up to a girl and ask her have sex with you, even though you don't know her, then you're a fuckboy."

"Whatever."

"You know I'm right. Admit it."

I ignored her and continued eating my food. She started to eat her food and we sat there for 30 minutes, not looking or talking to each other.

We went back to the room, and Ashley walked ahead of me. I could tell that she was really angry.

When we entered the room, she stomped into her room and slammed the door. Fuck. I gotta make this right.

I went to my room and grabbed her bikini and a cover up. It was a black cheeky bikini. It wasn't a thong, luckily. I knocked on her door a few times.

"GO AWAY!" She yelled.

"Ashley I need to talk to you. Open the door or I'm coming in." I gave her a few seconds and I heard the click of the door unlocking.

I walked in and she plopped on the bed with her arms crossed.

"What's wrong?"

"You're what's wrong. You act like you're the only one that's allowed to do anything. You kidnapped me so that you can have sex with me. But you get upset whenever someone looks at me or talks to me of the opposite gender. You act like there isn't a guy out there that's gonna love me for who I am. You make me feel that they only want what's in between my legs. And I don't know if you're jealous or what. Because I've told you multiple freaking times that Chase and I aren't dating. But you always bring it up. Am I not allowed to have any male friends or something? If not, then you should call my best friend Taylor and she can hang out with me. Oh wait, people think I've died or something." She kept going on and on about what was the matter. I wasn't listening, I was too busy focused on how cute she looked when she was angry or how plump her lips are. I would love to kiss those lips, bite them and have my name being moaned out from them. I noticed she was finished and she looked like she was about to cry. Her face was red and her eyes were watery. I scooted closer to her and lifted her onto my lap. She didn't try to push me away. I hugged her tightly and inhaled her scent. It smelt like vanilla and flowers.

"I'm sorry Ashley. I'm so sorry." I meant every word of that apology. She looked up at me and sniffled. "I brought your bikini and cover, so we could go to the pool if you're still interested."

She nodded. She got off my lap and grabbed the bikini off the bed, then proceeded into the bathroom. I sat on the bed, waiting for her to come out and show me what she looks like. It took her a while to get changed. I think she's trying to calm down and clean her face off. The door opened and there stood a sexy Ashley.

She was breathtaking and I could feel my cöck getting hard. She opened her arms and spun around slowly.

"So... How do I look?" She walked out the bathroom and pretended to act like a model. She didn't have to pretend to be a model, because I thought she always looked beautiful.

"You look... sexy, stunning, beautiful. I don't know enough words to describe how nice you look." She blushed at my comment. My eyes trailed up and down her gorgeous body. Over her ample breasts, her flat stomach, her somewhat thick thighs, her toned legs and feet.

"Aren't you gonna get dressed?" She snapped me out of my trance. I nodded and stood up abruptly. I rushed to my room, so that I can relieve this pent up tension. I put on my swim trunks and draped a towel around my neck. I walked out of my room to see Ashley sitting on the couch waiting for me. She had put her cover up on and had her towel on her lap. She also had some black slides on and that's it. I went and got my slides and we were out the door.

When we got to the pool, there were quite a few people there. A lot of men compared to the amount of women.

"Hey Ashley, do you want anything to drink?" I asked her before I head off to the bar.

"Uhh. Sure. Why not?" She followed me to the bar and sat beside me. The man behind the counter saw her and winked. I felt my jaw clench and my hands ball into fists. Ashley must've sensed something was wrong because she grabbed my hand and held onto it.

"What's wrong now?" She asked me.

"Nothing." I didn't want to tell her that I was jealous or really possessive of her. The bartender walked to where we were sitting and smiled.

"What might I get a beautiful woman such as yourself?" I cleared my throat and sent the guy a death glare.

"I'll have a Sweet Poison Cocktail." I looked over to Ashley so she could voice her order. She leaned over and whispered in my ear.

"I've never ordered alcohol before." I chuckled and decided to start her off with something delicious and light.

"She'll have a Blue Hawaii." The guy nodded his head and walked away.

"Why haven't you ever ordered an alcoholic beverage before."

"Because I'm only 18."

I nodded my head. I'm surprised she's never drank at all. The guy came back with our drinks a few minutes later and sent Ashley a wink. Ashley luckily ignored him and went to find ourselves a chair to put our stuff at. We found 2 lounge chairs and put our stuff down and made our way to the pool. Ashley handed me her drink so she could get in first. After she got in I handed her both of our drinks and got in. I stood next to her and watched her sip her drink.

"This is really good!" She said with a smile.

"Did you think that I would get you something bad?" She shrugged her shoulders. We finished our drinks and brought our glasses back to the bar to get more drinks.

"I want something stronger." She said.

"Are you sure that you can handle your alcohol?"

She nodded excitedly.

"Can we have a Sex on the Beach and a Screwdriver?" The bartender nodded. He got busy on our drinks. Ashley looked at me confused.

"Hmm. Why did you order a drink with sex in its name? And another that's called a screwdriver?"

"You know. I've never had sex on the beach before. I've had the drink just never the pleasure." I sent her a wink and a smile. She blushed and her eyes went wide.

The bartender set our drinks in front of us and we drank at the bar. Ashley downed her drink pretty fast for someone who's never drank before.

"Slow down Ashley, you don't want to be drunk."

"Why not? It's not like I do this often." She ordered herself some shots and I just sat back and watched. After 4 shots we went back to the pool to swim a little. She wasn't overly drunk, just a little drunk. She showed me that she could do flips and handstands under water.

"Ya know. I've always wondered if boys' dicks float when they go in the water." I scrunched up my eyebrows. All of a sudden she pulled at the band of my trunks and looked at my hard dick. I grabbed her wrist and tugged her hand off of my trunks.

"Don't do that Ashley." I said sternly. She grunted and got out of the pool and walked to the bar. I went after her. But the time I got there, she had 4 more shots in front of her.

"Watch what I can do." She downed the 4 shots in less than a minute and 30 seconds.

"Ashley. Let's go." I said sternly.

"You always.." she poked at my chest. "Boss me around. Like I'm a maid or somethin'." She slurred her words. People were starting to look at her.

I grabbed her arm forcefully and went over to the lounge chairs to get our stuff. She put her flip flops on, but not her cover up. I pulled her up and walked her back to our room.

"Let go of me. I can walk by my damn self."

Once we got into our room, I lightly shoved her inside.

"Go take a shower." She stumbled into her bedroom to presumably take a shower. I went into my room to do the same. When I stepped out of the shower, I put on some joggers and that's it. I got in bed. All of a sudden, Ashley bursts through my door with just a towel on.

"What the fuck Ashley."

She dropped the towel and walked towards my bed.

"Go to your fucking room."

"No. I know you want me. I know you want to do dirty things to me. Now's your chance." She crawled into my bed.

"I'm not fucking you while you're drunk. So go back to your room and go to sleep."

"You know what your problem is. It's that you say you like me and you get mad whenever someone treats me nicely. But you never treat me nicely or do what Chase does. You go and fuck that Barbie ass bitch right after you and I shared a moment. Like what the fuck. You went and bought her stuff, you don't ever do that to me and you expect me to like you."

"You don't like me?"

"I mean. I like you. You're so fucking hot. But, you treat me like shit and I don't like that."

"So what do you suggest I do, to win you over?"

"I don't know. Compliment me all the time. Buy me things, hold me, do fun stuff with me, chill, hold my hand, flirt try to get somewhere with me. Claim me."

"Claim you. How?"

"Kiss me out of nowhere, pick me up, give me hickeys, grab my butt anything."

"Ok. Are you done letting all of your emotions go?"

"See? This is exactly what I'm talking about. You're a jerk. If I had done this to Chase, he probably would've gave me a hug and apologized for how he was treating me. I mean, he wouldn't have to apologize because he treats me like a princess."

"Bye Ashley. You can leave." I was angry at her. She compared Chase and I, and I despise that. She huffed and stormed out of my room. To be completely honest, seeing her fully naked was a sight to see. She had the body that you would only find on a goddess. Her curves, her breasts, her shaven pûssy. It was all perfect. I got up and went to the bathroom and jacked off. I couldn't stay hard like this. After finishing my business. I checked in with the restaurants and with Emilio and Sam to make sure that business is booming and running smoothly.

Emilio told me that the guy that owed us $17,000, had finally paid, but since it took him forever to do so, he had to pay us 25 grand.

I put my laptop away and laid in bed just thinking. If I really want Ashley to be mine, I guess I'm going to show her and the world that she's mine and only mine.

(A/N) so I didn't want to move into the big house anymore. Because I found an even bigger house and it's more beautiful and ugh. I love it. And an update on my relationship status, still single but one guy likes me and I like a totally different dude sooo yeah.

Adios muchachos!

(21) What Happened?

☐ ☐ WARNING, THIS CHAPTER HAS A LOT OF SEXUAL CONTENT. CONTINUE IF YOU CHOOSE.

Ashley's POV

I woke up with a killer headache and naked. Oh shit. What the fuck happened last night. I sat up and went to grab some clothes from the closet and then went into the bathroom. I left the lights off, because my headache worsened whenever there was light. I brushed my teeth and walked out of my room. Kyle was on the couch working on his laptop. He was shirtless like always and only had some grey joggers on. I thought maybe he could clear things up for me.

"Good morning Kyle." I said groggily.

"Good morning beautiful." He smiled at me.

"Umm. What happened last night and do you have any pain medicine?" He got up and went to his room and came back with a bottle of Advil. As he walked towards me, I could see his whole body. What really caught my attention was in his crotch area. He was pretty hung. I could see a slight imprint of his dick, and when he walked it would swing. My eyes snapped back to his face when he cleared his throat and had a smirk on his face.

"Here, take this." He handed it to me and sat back down on the couch. "And for what happened last night. Well.. let's just say it was eventful."

"Did we.. I mean ya know?" I asked. I mean, I did wake up naked, so that was a relevant question.

"No we didn't, but you sure wanted to." I sat down next to him. Kinda shocked at what he said.

"What do you mean 'I sure wanted to'?"

"Well let's say you got really drunk. Then we got back, you took a shower and then walked into my room naked. Then asked me to fuck you while I had the chance."

"And you didn't.. ya know, take advantage of me?"

"Do you think I'm some sort of a monster? If anything, when you submit yourself to me. You're going to be sober, horny and head over heels for me. But, I don't do love, so you'll end up heartbroken." I gulped at his response.

My stomach growled, breaking the silence that was being held.

"I'll order some breakfast. Is there anything you particularly want?"

"Scrambled eggs with cheese, french toast with sugar, bacon and orange juice." Kyle got up and walked to his room, most likely to order our breakfast.

I walked back into my room and laid in the bed. 'Why'd you do that to yourself Ashley', I thought to myself. I groaned out loud and the bedroom door opened. Kyle walked in and plopped down next to me in the bed. He looked me over. I was wearing a velvet crop top and some pajama shorts with nothing underneath. He licked his lips which made me think about that time he kissed me.

I bit my lip. He moved his body so that it was above mine. His arms were on either side of my head. He lowered his face towards mine and claimed my lips with his. It was a forceful and lustful kiss, that made the spot between my legs tingle and me feel warm. I felt his tongue pressing against my lips demanding for entry. And surprisingly, access was granted because his tongue plunged into my mouth and explored. My tongue caressed his. He rolled us over, so I was on top. I felt his hands move to my hips and press down. I was so caught in the moment, that I didn't even know I was grinding into his growing hard erection. He groaned and bit my lip. He kissed me once more before stopping.

"We should probably stop before it gets too far and I'm unable to control myself. Also, we don't want the person delivering our food to hear you moaning and screaming." He winked.

He sat up and I was now in his lap with my legs wrapped around him. His large dick was poking at my butt and it was making me wetter by the minute. If I didn't get up soon, he would probably see that where my vagina and his crotch met, there would be a wet spot. He picked me up and walked out my room, with me still wrapped around him. He sat me on the counter on the kitchen and starting sucking and nibbling on my neck. I moaned and I could feel his smile against my neck. There was a knock on the door and he stopped doing what he was doing to answer the door. He answered it and I could hear the woman stuttering. I giggled. I heard the door close and Kyle walked up to me with a tray of food.

"Do you want to eat in my room or your room?'

"Yours." I said. I could feel my cheeks heat up, which only meant that I'm blushing. He carried the tray with our food and drinks to his room and I followed behind him. I sat in his bed, which smelt like him. Hmm Ashley,

I wonder why. It was an intoxicating smell that I just couldn't get enough of. He sat the tray on the bed and then sat down. He lifted the lids and we saw and smelt our delicious food. We ate in a comfortable silence. I walked into his bathroom for a quick second. Because he kept staring at me and smiling. I saw 2 hickeys on my neck.

"Why did you do this Kyle?" I said from the bathroom. I don't know if I'm admiring this thing or figuring a way to hide it.

"Do what Princess?"

"These marks." I walked out the bathroom and pointed to the hickey on my neck and right above my collarbone.

"To make sure that you know you're mine." He got up from the bed and hugged me. His hands were squeezing my butt and he was staring into my eyes. He lowered his head and started kissing me again. My hands were placed against his chest as he possessively took over my lips. He broke the kiss and smiled. "I think you already know." He grabbed the tray and walked out the room. I just stood there dumbfounded. I walked out of his room and he was walking towards it.

"What do you want to do today?" I shrugged my shoulders. "Well you can always go to the spa, you can go to the pool, they have engaging classes."

"I wanna go to the spa." I said quickly.

"Ok."

"I want you to come with me."

"What am I supposed to do at a spa? Get my nails done?" I shrugged. I grabbed his hand and observed his nails.

"I mean you can use a manicure. And if you come, I'll play the game that I'm playing with Chase, with you."

He scrunched up his eyebrows. "What game?"

I looked at him as if he was stupid. "You know what game."

"Is it the one where we play truth or dare?"

"No. I'm gonna call you daddy and you have to give me a cute nickname. Ok?"

"What kind of nickname?"

"I don't know. Like Baby girl, Princess, Sweetcheeks, Beautiful, and so on."

"Ok. I'm game. Let's go to the spa baby girl." I liked hearing Kyle saying baby girl to me. I don't know, it sounded better coming from him, than it does when Chase says it.

I went to my room and picked out a black short, flowy skirt since I wanted to wear the velvet crop top. The skirt was kinda sheer, but it didn't matter to me. I also wore some white converse and my gold earrings.

I walked out of my room and Kyle was standing in the kitchen waiting for me. He had a white polo on with black shorts and some Sperrys. He looked me over and licked his lips. I know what that meant. He stalked over to me like a predator does to its prey and he grabbed the sides of my face and started kissing me aggressively. I was just starting to notice how tall he was compared to my height. I'm 5' 3" and he had to be at least 6' 3". I kissed him back, our lips moving in sync, which was the perfect harmony. He nibbled on my lip and I let out a small moan. He let go of my lip and smiled. He backed off and my face was heated. I could feel my panties clinging onto the lips of my pussy which was slightly annoying. I couldn't go commando, but I could always change.

Kyle's hand went down to my butt and started rubbing and squeezing it. I was smiling and probably blushing really hard. A confused look came across Kyle's face and his hands stopped moving.

"Are you wearing panties Baby girl?" I nodded. Why wouldn't I be wearing panties? He dropped down onto his knees and looked up at me.

"Lift up your skirt." He demanded. What was he about to do? I could feel my heart beating faster and harder because I didn't know what to expect.

"Why?"

"I'm only going to ask once more. Lift up your skirt." My hands slowly made their way to the hem of the skirt. I swallowed down the fear and slowly lifted up the skirt. Kyle smiled.

"Why are you wearing underwear?" He stared at the wet spot in my underwear that my moistness has made.

"Because this skirt is really short, sheer and I'm supposed to wear underwear." I said as if he has asked me a dumb question. Which it really was.

"I'm going to take it off ok?" He started kissing my thighs and on top of my mound. This was causing me to get even wetter, and I had no doubt that he knew, and he could smell me. I moaned and he took that as a yes.

His fingers ran up my legs and went to the waist band of my panties and hooked onto them. He pulled my panties down while looking into my eyes. While I stared into his eyes, it reminded me of the ocean, I was getting lost in the ocean, known as his eyes. Once my panties were down, he kissed the lips of my pûssy and then gave them a quick lick. Seeing and feeling him do this to me reminded me of the time he ate me out. It was the best feeling ever. He stood up. His hand went to my pûssy and his fingers traced the lips. He found my clît and started to rub it. I moaned and my head fell back slightly. He would speed up then slow down, and I was getting wetter by the second. He stopped and I looked at him confusingly. His lips covered mine. I felt his fingers at the opening of my vagîna and felt him pushing one in. I gasped, but his lips were quick to cover mine again. His finger started moving in and out me if slowly. I started to moan and he smiled. He started kissing my neck and my collarbone which was turning me on more. I felt him add another finger and he started moving them faster and I was moaning uncontrollably. The he stopped. He pulled his fingers out of my vagîna and stopped leaving his marks all over my skin. I looked at him confusingly once again. He brought his fingers to his lips and tasted me.

"As sweet as last time." He cleaned of his fingers with a towel and grabbed my hand. We were about to leave.

"Daddy." He turned around and looked at me, shocked to hear that come out my mouth. "I was so close."

"I know Baby girl. I'll finish you off when we get back." We left the room and made our way to the spa. I was careful not to allow my skirt to be blown up by wind, and careful that it wouldn't show my butt. We got to the spa and the people got started on us right away. We first got a mani and pedicure. Then we got massages, then we sat in the mud bath. After the we were done, I felt so relaxed. I wasn't wet anymore, but I was still somewhat horny. And Kyle didn't make it any easier by teasing me.

When we left the spa, there was an announcement that we had docked in the Bahamas and we were able to leave the ship.

"Wanna go explore the Bahamas?" Kyle asked me as he held my hand. We were currently walking back to our room.

"Yeah, as long as I'm not drinking." Kyle laughed at my response. We got into the room and Kyle sighed really loudly. I turned to look at him. "I've been waiting to do this. He picked me up and started kissing me. He walked us into his room, but didn't stop. He tossed me onto the bed and had a lustful look upon his face. I was nervous, I knew what was about to happen, since it's happened before.

****

Kyle and I laid in the bed together. My naked body was against his half dressed body. I was under his arm, and my back faced him. When he ate me out, it was mind blowing. I came twice and squirted once. I'm still shocked at what he could do with my body. I felt him start kissing the back of my neck.

"Baby girl, you're awake." He sounded shocked. I mean, we did end up falling asleep after he ate me out, and we were asleep for about 2 hours.

"Mhmm." Laying down with him made me think of all the possibilities that could potentially happen. Like him and I dating or possibly even falling in love. Well, he says he doesn't do love, but there's always that one woman that can change a man. Well, there are in a lot of Wattpad stories anyway. And it's not like I'm the woman that's going to change him.

I thought about everything for a while. He treats me so nicely and I felt as if I should repay him. I turned around and kissed him. Then, I slid my body under the covers to where his waist was. I could see that he was hard, and I felt it earlier. I tugged his shorts down, and he wiggled a little to get it past his butt. I licked the tip and then spit on it. I used my hand to stroke his long dïck. I heard him moan. I guess I'm doing something right. The covers flew over my head and Kyle was staring down at me. I winked and then put my mouth on his cöck. I swirled my tongue around the head and licked the underside of his member. I started to bob my head up and down faster, and he let out a groan. I felt one of his hands on the back of my head, using a little bit of force and pushing me down. I tried to deep throat his dïck, but it was way too big. I went as far as I could go, but there was still 4 or 5 inches left. I held it in my mouth, then started bobbing my head up and down his dick. After a few minutes, I felt him shoot his load in my mouth and I swallowed it like a champ. He reached down and pulled me up. I was laying on his body and he was stroking my back. We were both naked and it didn't bother me.

"I thought you said this was never going to happen again." I looked up and saw a smile on his face.

"Well, things happen." I thought back to the day I said that to him, and how angry he got at me. Then I thought back to earlier this morning when he left those marks on me. I decided that the best way to get revenge was to do the same thing to him. I started kissing his chest and sucked, I'm not sure how long you need to do it for, since I've never gave anyone a hickey before. After I released his skin, there was a small pinkish-purple spot. I moved up to his neck and did the same thing.

"Baby girl, what are you doing?"

I released his skin, and smiled. "Nothing." He grabbed my ass then lightly spanked it. I yelped, not because of pain, but because that surprised me. I stopped kissing him and looked at my work. It was pretty good. I giggled and rolled off of him.

"I'm gonna go take a shower." I walked out of his room and to my room. I wasn't embarrassed while I was naked in front of him. He obviously likes my body, so what's to be ashamed of. I turned on the water in the shower and stepped in. I started singing while I washed my body until a pair of arms wrapped around me, startling me. I felt him kiss my neck and hold me. I pulled myself out of his embrace to continue washing my body.

"I think I need to be washed down too." He winked. I rolled my eyes and continued washing myself off. After I was finished with myself, I washed his body. His beautiful eyes monitored my motions on his body. As I washed his body, I admired it. It was like he was sculpted from God himself.

His perfect abs, his pecs, his broad shoulders, his muscles, and I cant forget about his amazing dick. I put some soap on my hand and stroked his semi-hard dick. He groaned and stared at me. He got hard pretty quickly. I decided I wasn't gonna finish him off. I turned the water off and he looked at me confused.

"Baby girl. I think you're forgetting about something." He looked down at his dick.

"I don't think I am." I stepped out the shower and grabbed a towel. He came out after me and grabbed a towel for himself.

"So, I'm supposed to walk around with a hard-on?" I smiled and nodded. He walked to his room, I'm guessing to relieve himself. I got dressed. More like I put on a bodysuit and that's it. I checked the time on my iPod, it was currently 5:15 pm. I decided that we might as well go explore the Bahamas before we leave tomorrow at 1 pm. I put a short bodycon dress on, with some lace up heels. I put on the choker that Chase got me and some earrings. I put my hair in a messy bun and walked out of my room into Kyle's.

"Can we go out tonight?" He was laying in his bed on his phone. He looked me over and licked his lips. I know what that meant, but since he's laying down, I'm hoping he won't get up.

"Come here." I walked over to him. He grabbed my wrist and pulled me on top of him. He started kissing me and grabbing my butt. He took a break from kissing me. "Are you wearing underwear?" I shook my head no. I sat up and my butt was on his crotch. He lifted his hands and grabbed my breasts. He rubbed his thumbs over my nipples, and they got hard. He smiled. I bit my lip at the pleasure he was giving me.

"Sooo... Can we go out?" He nodded his head. I got off his lap and stood back up. I went to my room and grabbed my chap stick, iPod, and earbuds.

I walked into the living room and waited for him to come out. He had dress pants, a dress shirt, a tie and some fancy shoes on. He even had a beautiful diamond watch on. He rolled up the sleeves on his shirt, which made him look 10x hotter.

"Let's go Princess."

(22) The Beach

☐ WARNING THIS CHAPTER CONTAINS VERY SEXUAL CONTENT. PROCEED AT YOUR RISK

Kyle's POV

I woke up with Ashley laying next to me in my bed. My arms were wrapped around her small frame and her back was facing me. Yesterday was great. I got to eat her out again and she sucked my dick. I love eating her out, she tastes wonderful. Like honey and fruit almost. When we went out last night, we went to dinner and walked around. We bought a few things and took some pictures. I remember grabbing her ass a lot, and kissing her. We held each other's hands and laughed plenty.

What the actual fuck is happening to me? I've never done shit like this with anyone and had a good time. With Cristina, all I want to do is leave, and with other women, I just want to fuck them. But with Ashley, I want to make her smile, please her, have fun, etc. What is she doing to me? I looked at her back. She wasn't naked, but she was just as beautiful. Fuck. I can't do this love shit in my kind of business. I just can't. And I'm pretty sure I'm falling in love with Ashley.

She moved a little bit. She turned her head slightly and looked at me.

"Good morning Daddy." She winked. I chuckled. What the hell.

"Good morning Princess." I kissed the back of her neck and sucked it a little. It left a little hickey, I'm pretty sure she won't mind though. She turned all the way around so that she would be facing me.

"What are we doing today?" She yawned. Wow, she's fucking adorable. I need to stop feeling this way towards her, because I don't want her to get hurt in the end or possibly die. I have to remember one thing; that my goal in the end is to fuck her brains out.

"Well the next place we're going to is the Dominican Republic. We should be there around 6:30 or so."

She looked so excited. "Can we go to the beach? I really want to watch the sunset."

"Sure." I happily agreed. I love seeing her smile. I grabbed the sides of her head and kissed her. It was a slow kiss, a lot different from the other kisses I've given her. This one was passionate, and delicate. I was able to feel her soft, plump lips.

"I think you should go brush your teeth." I broke apart the kiss. Her breath didn't smell bad since she brushed her teeth last night, but it didn't smell or taste the best. She groaned and got up. I laughed at her laziness. She looked so sexy. She was wearing one of my shirts and a pair of underwear. "Get dressed too, we're going to the dining hall for breakfast." The 2 floors below us and our floor had breakfast scheduled at 9:30 am to 10:30. I went to my closet and put some clothes on. I decided with some white basketball shorts and a black tee. I paired it with some Nike Elite socks and slides. Ashley came out my closet and looked me over. She went to her room and a few minutes later was in the living room dressed. She was wearing one of those black tee shirt dress thingys and some white converse.

"I'm starving." She said. Hinting me to hurry up.

"If you were so hungry, you could've asked me for some sausage." I winked at her.

"You're so immature." She giggled. We left to breakfast.

****

For the rest of the day, we went to a sushi making class and the pool. After that, we just chilled in the suite, watching Netflix. There was an announcement, telling us that we have finally made it to the Dominican Republic and that we would be leaving at 2 pm the next day. I glanced at my phone to check the time, when the sun would be setting, and the temperature for this evening.

It's currently 6:35 pm. We had an hour and 45 minutes until the sun started to set and the weather would be in the high 70s, so we were perfectly fine.

"Baby girl, get dressed. We're going out to dinner."

"What should I wear?" I sent her a mischievous smile and walked into her room. I chose a white bralette and a white skirt with white heels. I wore some navy pants and a white fitted tee shirt. I paired it with my Classima 8485 by Baume &Mercier. I also wore my black dress shoes. I planned on coming back to the ship before going to the beach. We walked off the ship and found a taxi to drive us into the city. We eventually found a restaurant, a beautiful one at that. The people in the front looked Ashley and I up and down as if we weren't able to afford it. They eventually seated us. Ashley got her usual Sprite and I got wine. I ordered a steak, and Ashley ordered fried fish, rice and beans and plantains. I've never had a plantain before and I didn't know what it was.

"So what are plantains?"

"They're a type of banana that you're supposed to cook before eating it. Like you can boil it, fry it, or saute it."

"You've eaten them before?"

She nodded her head. "Yeah Taylor's parents are from Haiti and they made plantains a few times. The first time I tried it, I fell in love." She seemed a little sad after talking about her best friend. She hasn't seen her for a little over a month.

"Sounds good. Are you gonna share with me?"

She looked like I just offended her. "Get your own plantains, I'm not sharing." Our food came out and we ate.

•••

Ashley's POV

We walked back to the cruise ship after eating. It was a really great dinner and I couldn't wait to go to the beach. Kyle stole some of my plantains so I refuse to talk to him until I get more plantains, of course he doesn't know that, because I'm not talking to him. When we got to the room, it was 7:50. Kyle rushed around getting stuff in a bag. Like blankets, food, drinks and two pillows. While he did that, I changed my shoes, so that I would be wearing slides. He called a cab to come take us to the beach.

A little while later we finally arrived at the beach. It was a gorgeous sight to see, and the sun was just starting to set. We were at a secluded part of the beach and there were a few big rocks to the side of us. Kyle quickly laid a big blanket down, I'm guessing it belonged to one of the beds, and he put the pillows on top of the blanket. I sat down, and he sat down next to me. I sat patiently, watching the sun slowly set. It relaxed my mind, I listened to the waves, the people, the birds, the wind. I just admired everything.

"Ashley, what's wrong? Did I do something?" I laid down, onto my pillow and just stared at the sky. I pretended as if I never heard his question. He positioned his body over mine, not letting his body weight crush me though. I looked at him with an annoyed expression. He dipped down and kissed me on my lips, but I wasn't kissing back. He moved to my neck, and started kising me and probably leaving hickeys. He kissed my chest, not too close to my boobs though. "I'm sorry." He didn't even know why he was apologizing. He kissed my shoulders and my face. I moaned a few times when he would nibble and suck on my skin.

He looked to see if my expression had changed, him kissing me didn't work that much. He got off of me and went down to where my legs were. He pulled off my panties and I did nothing to stop him. He looked back up at me, our eyes met, but I quickly reverted them to the sky. He started kissing my inner thighs and my mound. I was moaning a lot more.

"I'm." *kiss* "Sorry" *kiss* "For whatever" *kiss* "I" *kiss* "Did" he kissed me one last time. He started licking my pûssy, causing it to get wetter and wetter. He started to suck and finger me too. I was starting moan louder and louder. I quickly sat up. I accepted his apology, and I also didn't want to become a moaning mess on a beach.

He looked up at me shocked. "Did I do something wrong?" I smashed my lips onto his. We made out, which caused us to be laying down on the blanket. He was on top of me and my back against the ground. My hands went down to the edge of his shirt and pulled it off of him. Then, I unbuttoned and unzipped his pants. My hands weren't able to go any lower than that. He stopped kissing me. I looked into his eyes. It was dark outside, but not too dark. I could still see the blue in his eyes and they looked a little darker.

"Are you sure Baby girl?" I nodded and bit my lip. I didn't know what I was signing myself up for, but I was ready to find out. He went back to kissing me, lust and hunger consumed him. My fingers ran through his hair while he scooted the skirt off of me a little. He stopped kissing me, so that he could strip me down and strip himself. Once we were both naked, I knew there was no going back. I stared at his long cöck and felt nervous, yet extremely horny. He walked closer to me and I sucked on his cöck. I tried deep throating his dïck, but it was just way too big. After it was wet enough for his liking he kneeled in between my legs and looked at me for one more confirmation. I nodded. I saw him clench his jaw, trying to go easy on me. Little did he know, that my hymen was broken by a dildo that I had bought online. I felt his thick cöck align at my entrance. I felt the pressure as he pushed the head into my slit. It hurt a little, since I haven't had something this big ever go in there. He pushed in a little further and stopped. I saw a confused look on his face. I bit my lip. He leaned towards me and kissed me while pushing the rest of his length inside me. His kiss was passionate and distracted me from the slight pain in my pûssy as I accommodated his size. After a little bit, he broke the kiss and pulled out slowly. Not allowing the head to slip out and he slowly pushed back in. He groaned. I could see how hard it was for him to take his time.

He started speeding up and I started moaning and screaming. My hands found their way to his back and tried pulling him closer towards me, I'm assuming they might leave scratches.

"You're so fucking tight. Fuck!" He moaned as he fucked me. I became a moaning mess and I was starting to scream his name.

"KYLE...Yes yes yes. Uh, FUCK ME. FUCK ME HARDER!" He smiled and started kissing me forcefully. He rolled himself onto his back, his dïck never leaving me.

"Let me see you fuck yourself Baby girl." His hands landed on my hips, as he laid back and watched me bounce desperately on his cöck. You could hear our skin slapping together, the wetness of my pûssy, our loud moaning and screaming. He told me to slide off of him quickly.

"Get on your hands and knees." I followed his order quickly.

He slid into my pûssy slowly from behind. I gasped at this position, it felt so good. He started fucking me again. I felt his hand go to my messy bun that had somewhat come undone. He started pulling my hair slightly. His other hand moved around me and found my clît. He started massaging my clît.

"C'mon Ashley. Let me see you cum." He moaned.

The pain and the pleasure was too much and I started to cum.

"I'M CUMMING!!!" I screamed loudly. He started moving in and out faster and my pûssy was clenching and releasing on his dïck. He slammed into my one last time and I felt his warm cum shoot inside of me. As my orgasm died down I fell onto the blanket and so did he.

"We should probably start heading back." I nodded. I got up and started getting dressed. As I got dressed, it finally dawned on me that Kyle had cum in me. I wasn't on the pill either, oh shit. I'm definitely not ready to be a mother, and I don't want a kid with Kyle. It's okay, I'll just wake up really early tomorrow and go to the store to get the morning after pill.

(A/N) SO THEY FINALLY HAD SEX?!?! I liked writing this chapter. I honestly couldn't wait to type the sexual scene. I hope y'all liked it.

Anyway, I've attracted more guys, but I realized that I'm not ready for a relationship. And also cause these guys are on too many games.

Keep reading, vote and comment. Ciao for now!

(23) Emotions

Kyle's POV

I woke up the next day around 4 in the morning. I had to sneak out of the room because last night after having sex on the beach with Ashley, we came back and showered together, then fell asleep in the same bed. But, I had to sneak out because she never said anything about being on any birth control or anything of the sort, and I came in her. So there's a problem. I don't need a baby, nor do I want one. I reached my goal and I'm happy now. I got to fuck Ashley. I was inside the closest pharmacy looking for the morning after pill, so I could give it to Ashley. I found a pretty good one and bought it. I went back to the ship and luckily she was still asleep. I filled a glass of water and left the pill and the water on the nightstand next to her. I leaned against the wall and watched her sleep. She was naked. Her breasts were covered by blankets, but her shoulders were exposed. She looked peaceful and so beautiful. Her hair was splayed on the pillow, making her look like she had a brown halo.

I made a mental note that when we get back, I need to get Ashley on some birth control pills if I'm going to continue fucking her. Her pûssy was the best I've ever been in. It was tight, warm, wet, soft, and was her cervix was deep enough where the tip of my dïck would lightly press it when I went all the way in. I wouldn't mind fucking her all the time.

I took all my clothes off, to match her nudity. I slipped back into bed and wrapped my arms around her. She moved herself towards me as I pulled her closer. I kissed her neck and drifted back to sleep.

•*•*•*•*•*•*•*•*•*•*•*•*•*•*•*•*•*•*•

Ashley's POV

I woke up really sore, naked and in Kyle's bed. I remembered what happened last night and I was shocked to say the least. I never wanted to have sex with Kyle, because he was the one who kidnapped me. I never wanted to have sex with Kyle because I wanted to be in love with that person before having sex and Kyle doesn't do love. I mentally groaned. I carefully got up and noticed there were pills and a cup of water on the nightstand. I grabbed it and read what it was. It was the morning after pill, he must've went and got it for me this morning. I grabbed it and took it to my room. I read the instructions and how it's supposed to work. I'll still probably go to the doctors when we get back to make sure I'm not pregnant. I went into the closet and luckily there were extra sheets, and I put those on the bed. I also got dressed and laid in bed, reminiscing about last night.

Sex with him was better than masturbating with a dildo. His dïck was a lot bigger and it could move itself in and out of me. It hit all the right spots and had me orgasming like never before. The way he moaned my name, and fucked me was beyond amazing. I still can't believe I let him do it though. I grabbed my iPod and started watching YouTube videos. I heard a knock on my door and Kyle walked through it before I said anything. He was wearing basketball shorts without anything under it. I could tell because his morning wood was swinging around.

"Good morning beautiful." He laid on the door of my bed. "Why'd you leave me?"

I looked away from his eyes. I didn't want to say that I'm embarrassed or that last night was a mistake. I didn't want to admit how great it was and that I wouldn't mind doing it again. I mentally sighed and looked him in his eyes.

"Good morning." I smiled, trying to get away from his question.

"Are you going to answer my question?"

I shrugged my shoulders and looked at my hands. I started looking at my painted nails and admiring how beautiful they are. He got up and groaned.

"Ashley, did I do something wrong? Why aren't you talking to me?" He ran his fingers through his hair.

I felt bad for making him worry, I guess I better answer him. "No. You didn't do anything wrong." Maybe that would make him feel better.

He got into the bed, right next to me. "Then why did you leave me? Why aren't you speaking to me?" He spoke quickly. His eyes searched my face for a clue.

"I just.. I." I sighed, becoming frustrated. "Remember when I said I only wanted to have sex with someone I love? Why was it so easy for you to throw away my morals and have sex with me?" I felt as if I was going to cry. "Why did you have to kidnap me? Why are you so interested in me? Just look at me, I'm not extremely pretty or super skinny." I moved my hands along my body. He got up and stood at the bottom of my bed just watching me pour my heart out. "Why couldn't you have fucked some other girl?" I felt the tears streaming down my face. My face felt hot and I was so frustrated, all my pent up feelings being let out. "I mean. You were the first person to ever have sex with me. Ever. And you don't even like me.

All you wanted was to fuck me and you got that. Now what am I supposed to do? Are you going to ditch me in some country? Kill me?" I was actually scared and confused. I brought my knees up to my body and held them while I cried.

•••

Kyle's POV

Her crying made my heart feel like it was being stabbed. I felt bad for what I did to her. I sat beside her again and brought her body towards mine. I placed her on my lap and let her cry on me. I have no idea what came over me, I did know that I really wanted to comfort her. I stroked her back until her crying became hiccups. She leaned against me.

"I'm sorry Ashley. I'm sorry for everything. I'm sorry that I had sex with you and made you feel as if your morals were unimportant to me. I'm sorry that I took you from your normal life and forced you into mine. I'm sorry that I made you feel like an object that's only job was to pleasure me. I'm sorry that my first thought when I met you was that you were mine. I'm not sorry that I picked you out of all the females in the world. I'm not sorry for being so intrigued and curious about you. I saw you Ashley, and thought you were so beautiful. I did want to fuck you and kick you out at first. But after a while, you made me interested. I saw how beautiful you were inside and out. How seeing your smile made my day feel better. You think that you're not beautiful. But I think you're more than that. I think that you're beautiful, sexy, kind, strong, independent, and kinda goofy. Another thing that you got wrong was that I didn't like you. I haven't told you how much I like you. I mean you've probably seen how jealous I get when you and Chase are together, it's because I like you. It's because I don't want to have to share you with anyone else. The only reason that I don't want to tell you, is because it makes it real. You could end up getting hurt, and I don't want that to happen to you." I spoke to her from my heart. It was an interesting experience to say the least, since I'm not big on sharing my emotions with people.

She sniffled and looked up at me. Her tear stained face, red eyes, red face, and confused expression said a lot. It told me that I never wanted to see her like this ever again. "You mean that?" I nodded my head slowly. She wrapped her arms around me and gave me a tight hug. I loved it, it was comforting. It made me feel as if she appreciated me sharing my feelings and expressing myself. Honestly, I was kinda scared, but I have no idea why.

"I'm hungry." She said. She was still sniffling, because of her previous crying. I chuckled at how random that was.

"Ok... We could either go down for breakfast, we could go into the city or we could have breakfast delivered up here. What do you want?"

"Let's go down stairs for breakfast." She got off of me and went into her closet. I wanted to join her badly. I wanted to pick out her outfit, see her naked, and maybe even fuck again. But I figured out that she might need her space. I went into my room and put some army green cargo shorts on, a white shirt and my all white Nike Roshes. I sprayed on some cologne, and grabbed sunglasses, then headed out to the living room. Ashley soon walked out of her room in white denim booty shorts and a body suit that read "Property of No One." That irritated me a little since she knew how possessive I am over her. I sighed loudly and we left. She didn't talk to me, it was almost as if she was avoiding me. She had her earbuds plugged into her iPod an she was listening to music. Whenever I asked her a question, she wouldn't answer.

When we got to the cafe, we got a table and a waitress came to us quickly. She kept staring at me, while I stared at Ashley. I paid no attention the what the waitress was saying to me, because I was so focused on Ashley.

"Excuse me, Sir?" I snapped out of my trance and looked up at her. She was a blonde girl with red lipstick on. "Would you like to order your drinks?" I nodded.

"May I have black coffee?" I saw that Ashley was still not paying attention. I kicked her foot and she looked up at me, then at the waitress. The waitress wasn't paying Ashley any mind, just admiring me.

"May I have apple juice?" The waitress looked at her then mumbled something. I could barely hear her, it was something on the lines of "Ew" Yada yada "ugly little girl."

It caused me to get angry, but I didn't want to cause a scene here. Or cause a scene in front of Ashley, I didn't want her to see how ruthless and cold-hearted I could be. The waitress walked away, and Ashley was reading the menu. I was going to say something, but I thought the best thing I could do once again, was give her space. I chose to get a Belgium Waffle, scrambled eggs, and bacon. Ashley got French toast, eggs, and bacon.

When our food came out, I was so hungry. I dove right into my food. Ashley was eating, but still looking at her iPod. I wanted to know what she was doing, so I grabbed it from her hand.

"HEY. Give that back!" She raised her voice. The earbuds had fallen out her ears, when I took the iPod away.

"No." I double clicked the home button, to see what her most recent apps were. I saw messages, iMusic, Netflix and Youtube. I clicked on messages. I know for a fact that she wasn't texting me, so who the fuck was she texting. At the very top I saw 'Chase'. I lost it. First it was her attitude change, then the waiter and now she's talking to Chase after I told her how I felt!

I slammed the iPod onto the table. The screen cracked and Ashley was shocked and angry. She got up abruptly and stormed off. She had barely eaten her food, so I knew she was going to be hungry later. Luckily, I could still see what was being presented on the screen, despite the cracks. I read through the messages and I couldn't feel anymore angry. A lot of the messages that they sent each other made it look like they were in a relationship. Not only today's messages, but previous messages also. The ones from this morning really blew me.

C- Good morning beautiful A- Good morning C- How are you A- Eh I'm ok C- What happened??? A- It's Kyle. He made me really... A- idk C- Do I need to beat him up again? A- You would do that for me A- And no, you don't need to beat anyone up C- Ok, what are you doing A- Going to get breakfast C- You know what would be good for breakfast? A- What?? C- You A- I wouldn't know, I've never tried myself

She didn't shut him down, and say something like "That'll never happen" or "yikes". Like what the fuck. She knows she's mine and Chase knows that too, but I don't know why he won't get that through his thick skull. I left $40 on the table and left. I needed to blow off some steam, because I didn't want to accidentally hurt Ashley or do something that I'll regret. I decided to head to the fitness room, because they should have a punching bag, and luckily they did.

I started punching the bag without any gloves on, I needed to feel the pain. I needed something to distract me from this anger. People were staring at me as if I were crazy. I was punching the bag hard and fast. I took off my shirt, because I was starting to get hot. I chucked it onto the ground. I could feel people's gazes on me. I stopped punching the bag and looked at my knuckles. Fuck. They were red, swollen and bleeding. I picked up my shirt and walked out of the fitness room. I went back to the room and went into my room. I took a shower and cleaned my knuckles off. Ashley stormed into my room as I laid in bed and scrolled through Instagram.

"Give me back my fucking iPod." She said harshly. I shrugged my shoulders and kept looking at my phone. "Give it back."

"I can't, I broke it and threw it away."

"What the fuck is wrong with you?" She yelled at me. She was beginning to irritate me. I stood up and walked towards her. Her angered expression didn't change and she didn't seem intimidated by me. But she should be.

"You wanna know what's wrong? I told you how I fucking felt earlier, something I've never done. And you didn't fucking care. You wore that bodysuit thing on purpose. I told you that you were mine, but you didn't fucking listen. You were texting Chase, when I told you how exactly how that made me fucking feel. You just don't fucking listen and that pisses me off. I tried talking to you earlier and you ignored me as if I wasn't fucking there." I yelled at her. I could tell that she was scared because her expression changed from anger to shock. She also backed away from me while I was yelling, but I moved closer to her.

"I'm sorry." She whispered. She was looking down at the ground. I felt bad for yelling at her, but she made me angry. I turned around and got back into bed. I picked up my phone and started scrolling through Instagram again. She was still standing against the wall staring at me. She slowly inched towards me before she was beside me. She got on top of my lap and kissed me. She kissed me passionately. I put my phone down and grabbed onto her hips.

"I'm so sorry for making you angry." She kissed my neck softly and gave me a hug. I hugged her back and we sat there for a few minutes in each other's embrace. She let go of me and grabbed my hands.

"What happened?" She looked at my knuckles.

"I was beyond angry after you left, so I went to the fitness room and started punching the punching bag without gloves."

She lifted my hands up and kissed my knuckles. She got up and left my room. She came back a few minutes later with 2 bags of ice and a first aid kit. She cleaned my knuckles some more, which stung a little, applied some ointment and wrapped them. She put the bags of ice on my knuckles to help with the swelling. She climbed back onto my lap and looked into my eyes. I never knew that I could forgive someone so easily. I was no longer mad at Ashley.

"Sorry for yelling at you." She shrugged her shoulders.

"It's okay."

"It's not okay. I should never yell at you like that. I'm sorry that you had to see that side of me."

"I have a question."

"Okay?"

"If I'm yours, then am I your girlfriend, or fuck buddy. Because I definitely don't want to be your fuck buddy."

"Ashley Rowens. Will you be my girlfriend?"

(A/N) Sooo.... this guy who has anger issues likes me again. But I don't like him back, but he's a really nice guy. But he dated my friend and he's not really good looking. He's always coming to me with his problems, sooo yeah. Idk how to tell him that I'm not interested. I've done it before, he just doesn't listen.

Anyway.... KYLE ASKED ASHLEY TO BE HIS GIRLFRIEND AND IM SOOO HAPPY. LIKE IT ONLY TOOK YOU 23 CHAPTERS!!!

Adios, readers. I hope you're enjoying my book thus far and I hope you vote, comment and keep reading. Next chapter is on its way.

(24) We're back

Ashley's POV

Ever since Kyle asked me to be his girlfriend, he's been really sweet. I mean we've only been dating for 2 days. He holds my hand, kisses me, holds me, talks to me, we're like friends, but more. We haven't had sex since the time we did it on the beach. I was sitting on his lap kissing him, which was distracting him from getting his work done. I thought it was funny, but I don't think he was amused.

"You're going to need to get off now, so I can handle this situation at work." I pouted on his lap and he groaned. He grabbed the side of my face and started kissing me again. "Okay, can I get my work done?" I rolled off of his lap and sat next to him.

"So, did you tell Chase what time to pick us up tomorrow?" I asked him, while he typed away on his laptop.

"Shit. Uh no, I didn't. I've been distracted by someone." I pretended to act shocked.

"Who's distracting you? We need to tell them to stop." He chuckled and I laughed.

"You're not tired yet? It's.." He checked the time. "11:37 pm." I shook my head no. "Can you hand me my phone please?" I grabbed it and gave it to him.

He unlocked his phone and started texting someone, I assumed it was Chase.

"What color iPod do you want?"

"Uhh. Gold?"

"Okay." I was shocked that he was getting me an iPod. I knew he was rich, but he just replaces things like it's never going to make a dent in his bank account.

I yawned and laid down. "I'm tired, I'm going to sleep."

"Goodnight princess." He left the room, to give me peace and quiet while he handled business.

****

When I woke up, it was around 10:22 am. Kyle was beside me sleeping. I wonder what time he joined me. The ship was supposed to dock at 11:00 am. Oh crap! We have to get up and pack. I sat up and shook Kyle. He woke up slowly.

"Good morning Sleeping Beauty." His voice was raspy.

"Kyle, get up. We need to pack our clothes."

"Lay down."

"Kyle c'mon." I whined.

"I did it last night, come lay with me."

"What?" I was shocked, he packed everything by himself.

"Come here please." I got in the bed and kissed him. It was a really nice kiss, but we both needed to brush our teeth.

"We still need to get dressed, because I want to go eat when we get off." He groaned and I giggled. I got up and went to the bathroom. He didn't pack our toiletries so we could still use them in the morning. I started brushing my teeth and he came in. He grabbed his toothbrush and started brushing his teeth. When we finished, we got dressed and packed everything else. By the time we were done, we had docked and we could leave right away.

"Come here Ashley." I walked into his bedroom, thinking that I had left something behind.

"Yes?" He picked me up and pushed me against the wall then started kissing me. It was rushed and a lustful kiss. He then moved to my neck and left some new hickeys because the previous ones had faded.

"Remember who you belong to." He put me down.

"Uhh. Who was it? Oh yeah, no one." He groaned and slapped my butt.

"You belong to me, got it?" I nodded and smiled. We grabbed our stuff and headed out of the suite. We checked out and we were ready to go. Kyle called Chase while we waited outside.

I was looking around to see if I could find him. Then I spotted him. I waved and tapped Kyle's shoulder to let him know that I had found Chase. He hung up on Chase and stood up. Chase walked over to us and gave me a hug. I hugged him back because he was my friend and I haven't seen him in a week.

"Hey Ashley, long time no see." He said hi to Kyle and he grabbed our stuff. We walked to the car and I sat in the back. Chase was driving and Kyle was in the passenger seat.

I WANT HER

"So Beautiful, where do you wanna go for breakfast?" I saw the way Kyle glared at Chase when he asked me that question. I just remembered that Kyle gave me a whole bunch of hickeys. I bet he did that on purpose. It's a good thing that Chase hasn't seen them or else he's gonna be pissed.

"Hmm... IHOP!" I said and both men chuckled. I didn't think it was funny. I'm hungry, and bored because someone broke my iPod.

When we arrived at IHOP, it wasn't extremely busy, so we were seated in a good amount of time. We got a booth near the window which was really nice, since I had nothing better to do than look out of it. Kyle sat next to me and Chase sat right across from me. I felt Kyle's hand settle on my thigh which was a shock to me. It was beginning to make me feel a tingly sensation in my region and I couldn't do anything about it.

I looked up at Kyle who was acting like nothing was going on. I looked at the menu and already knew what I was going to get. "Ashley, I texted you last night, but you never responded." Chase broke the silence. I felt my face get hot, I had no doubt that my cheeks were red.

"Yeah..uh about that. My iPod broke, and I'm unable to use it." I looked out the window and looked at the sky.

"What's all over your neck?" He sounded kinda upset. I quickly turned my head to face him then I looked over at Kyle who was grinning. I knew he would eventually see them, I just wasn't prepared. I was too shocked to answer his question, I just sat there staring at him, while he glared at me.

"They're called hickeys. And I gave them to her." Kyle answered the question for me, and I was somewhat grateful. I didn't want to explain how I got hickeys or what they were.

"You what!?" Chase raised his voice. I felt Kyle's hand starting to slide up my thigh. He was enjoying this however, I most certainly was not.

"Yeah, you should've seen the stuff we did. I fucked her on the beach, we slept naked, we pleasured each other. Good times." I cleared my throat. Kyle didn't need to say all of that and he had no right to. That was supposed to remain private, and stay only between us. I was going to leave and go to the restroom, but the waitress came. She was checking out both Chase and Kyle.

"Would you like to start off with your drinks, or would you like to order?"

"Order." She nodded her head.

"May I have the breakfast sampler please, and scramble my eggs, with cheese. May I have coffee also?" Kyle went first.

The longer I stayed here, the more uncomfortable I became.

"May I have the split decision breakfast and scramble my eggs also, and I want them with cheese. With orange juice." Chase said with an attitude.

"May I have the quick two egg breakfast? Make the eggs scrambled with cheese and is it possible to have a waffle and bacon?" She nodded her head. "And an apple juice please." The waitress grabbed our menus and left. Chase was still glaring at me, but I did nothing wrong. It wasn't like we were dating or anything. I quickly got up, and walked to the ladies restroom.

I looked at myself in the mirror and just thought. Why have I changed? I used to be such a good girl and I had standards. Now, some boy just walks into my life and I allow him to fuck me? Seriously? If Taylor were here, she would be congratulating me for finally losing my virginity to a real person.

I sighed. I really miss Taylor and all my friends. I miss my family, I miss my new car and most of all, I really wanted to have an adventurous year with Taylor, and now I'm going to miss out on that. I felt the tears starting to run down my face. I walked into a stall and locked myself inside. I put a toilet seat cover down and sat on the toilet. I wasn't using it, I was just sitting there crying. Why am I such an emotional mess?

I'm going to ignore Kyle from now on. Because he had no right to tell Chase anything that we did intimately while we were gone. He could've asked if I was okay with him telling people, but I probably would've still said no. I got up from the toilet and flushed the cover down. I walked to the mirror and wiped my face with a paper towel. Then someone came into the bathroom. It was Kyle. I ignored him and washed my hands. Bathrooms are dirty you know.

"Ashley are you okay?" He grabbed my wrist as I tried to walk away from him.

"Let go of me." I said sternly. I tugged my wrist from his grip and walked out the bathroom. He quickly followed me out the bathroom. Chase was still there, but the food had yet to arrive. As we sat down the waitress came with our food. I dug into my food quickly because I was super hungry. The guys did the same. We didn't talk to each other, just ate. When we were done, Chase paid the bill and we left. When we got into the car, Chase asked me a question.

"Did you ever like me?" It took me by surprise. I'm guessing that while I was in the restroom, they talked about it and worked it out. I sighed.

"Yeah. I liked you a lot. I liked you more than I liked Kyle." Kyle turned and looked at me. "You were always nice to me, you're funny, and became my friend when I needed one."

"So why'd you choose Kyle?" He asked me. He still hasn't started driving. We were just sitting in the car, luckily the A/C was on.

"I don't know. At the gala, I realized I liked both of you, so I was just going to wait it out and see what happens. And spending that week with Kyle happened." I knew for a fact that Kyle had a huge smile on his face.

Chase started up the car and drove us to Kyle's penthouse. When we got there, it looked like it was recently cleaned. I brought my stuff to my room with the help of Chase. We then brought all my dirty clothes to the laundry room, so that I could wash them.

"Can we still be friends?" I nodded. I gave him a tight hug and laughed.

"Why wouldn't we be friends? You're awesome, and if I ever need to beat someone up, you'll help." I smiled and cracked my knuckles. He laughed and shook his head.

We walked out of my room and into the living room. Kyle was in there, I hadn't forgave him for what he did, so I'm still going to ignore him. I tapped Chase on the shoulder and told him to come down to my level. I stood on my tippy toes and whispered in his ear.

"We should go hang out." He chuckled. He turned and whispered into my ear.

"Where do you want to go?" I shrugged my shoulders. We both thought it was funny that I wanted to hang out, but I didn't know where I wanted to go.

"ASHLEY!" Kyle called out to me from the couch. "Come sit with me." I rolled my eyes and walked out of the pent with Chase. Once we got into the hallway, we started discussing the possible places we could hang out. The options were the movies, but I didn't know what movies were out. There was Sky Zone, but I wasn't really dressed for that, mostly because I had a t-shirt dress on. Also Chick-fil-a or the mall, but I didn't want Chase to buy me stuff because we aren't dating.

Once we got to the parking garage we were off.

(A/N) So one of the guys that like me saw that I made Christmas cookies (it was on my Snapchat story) so he asked for some. This guy is also my neighbor. So I said ok. I grabbed two cookies, my jacket and Ugg slippers. I put my jacket on and my slippers and let me tell you something. I was wearing a short t-shirt dress that ended like 2 inches below my butt, but I didn't put pants on cause I didn't feel like going all the way to my room to get pants, just to take them off. So I went to the backyard and he likes climbing the fence, so like from his hips up, was peering over the fence and the fence is about 6 feet high. He told me that he was smacked (high). I gave him the cookies and he tried them and he really liked them. He tried talking to me, but my legs were lowkey freezing, and I told him that they were. He was like "Nice legs, they're very long. They could be wrapped around me." And this kid winked. I walked back inside without responding. He snapped me later and was like "why did you leave" so I left him on opened.

Anyway.... I HATE WHEN GUYS TELL PEOPLE WHAT THEY DID INTIMATELY WITH A GIRL. LIKE THATS SUPPOSED TO BE PRIVATE @KYLE

Adios readers

(25) The Doctor's Visit

Ashley's POV

Chase dropped me back off at Kyle's penthouse and bid me good bye. I told him that I would somehow let him know if and when I get a phone or an iPod. We spent the day at the mall, chick-fil-a and the movie theater.

I walked inside and the penthouse was dark. I was confused as to where Kyle was, because I looked all around the penthouse and couldn't find him. I was unable to call him because he didn't have any house phones and I didn't have any communication devices. I would send him an email, but his office is always locked. I decided to just take a bath and watch Netflix. After the bath, I made myself some dinner. I made chicken tenders and french fries. I sat down and watched Orange is the New Black. I finished my dinner and brought my dishes to the sink, I'll just wash them tomorrow. I sat back on the couch and continued watching Orange is the New Black. I started getting tired, but I didn't feel like getting up from the couch, so I laid down on the couch, with my blanket and fell asleep. I didn't turn the TV off because I was watching it while falling asleep.

I woke up to a loud slam. I woke up scared and thinking that I was going to die. The TV was still on, so I turned it off and crept to where I thought the noise was sounded from. I saw Kyle trying to walk to his room and he smelt of alcohol.

"What the fuck?" He looked at me and then looked away. He tried walking to his room, but he was disorientated and stumbling. I tried helping him to his room, but he's really big and heavy compared to me. He leaned against me and started talking.

"You wanna know why I'm drunk?" He slurred his words. I nodded my head as we walked to his room.

"Because, I like you and that's just crazy. And Chase likes you. I bet you guys went somewhere and fucked." I let him plop onto his bed. I felt disrespected that he thought I would cheat on him. "He probably had you screaming like the little whore you are." I was infuriated, which ended up with me slapping him.

"DON'T EVER HIT ME BITCH!" He yelled at me. I was pretty shocked. "You think you're not a whore. But YOU, made the first move. YOU sucked my dick. Which makesss YOU a whore." He emphasized the word 'you'. I stormed out of his room and slammed my bedroom door. Unfortunately, there was no lock on the door. I got into bed and felt like screaming or crying, maybe even both. Why would I be a whore, why would I cheat on Kyle?

I went to sleep with a tear stained face.

****

I woke up, and went to the bathroom. As I did everything I needed to do in the bathroom, the event from last night replayed in my mind. It put me in a bad mood, and I definitely did not want to see Kyle. I decided to just stay in my room and tried my best to entertain myself. I looked out the window, put on a fashion show, sang and danced. Of course there wasn't any music, but a girl could dream. I was in the middle of singing my favorite song when I heard a knock on my door.

My door opened and his head peered inside. I got angrier. I threw my pillow at the door. "LEAVE ME ALONE." I yelled. I was hungry and angry already, I didn't need him to make it any worse than it already was. He opened the door fully and looked sad. "Do you not understand me? I said leave me alone." I raised my voice at him. He walked closer to my bed and sat at the foot of it.

"Look Ashley. I don't remember exactly what happened last night, but I can see that I made you extremely angry."

"Oh my gosh! Your eyes work? Does your brain? Cause you certainly don't use it." I said harshly.

He sighed. "I'm sorry for whatever I did to make you angry."

"Leave me alone until you figure it out." I could see him clench his jaw.

"Ashley. I can't leave you alone. I need you. I want you. Without you, I feel angry, ruthless and empty. With you, I feel happy, needed and loved."

"You certainly didn't think that last night. So leave."

"Ashley, I was drunk. I didn't mean anything that I said."

"Ya know. I once heard that when someone is angry or drunk, that's usually when they tell the truth about how they feel about people. Now leave me alone since you think I'm a cheating whore." I started getting really irritated with him being here.

"What?" He looked confused.

"I'll leave you alone once you tell me what I did last night that made you so angry."

I groaned loudly. I might as well tell him, because if I don't, he'll never leave me alone. So I told him, from the part where he woke me up by slamming the door, to the point where I walked out and slammed my door. He listened to what I was saying and I could tell he was shocked.

"I'm sorry for calling you a whore, and a bitch. I'm so sorry for yelling at you and hurting your feelings. I'm so sorry Ashley." He moved closer to me and tried to hug me. I pushed his arms away from me.

"I thought you said you would leave me alone if I told you everything. Why are you still here?" He sighed and stood up.

"Okay. But I want you to know that I like you a lot, and you're not going anywhere." He walked out of my room and the atmosphere felt light again. I felt less tense. I laid in my bed and just stared at the ceiling. Where did I go wrong? Why did I open the door for that stranger at night?

I smelt bacon being cooked and my stomach growled. Dang it. I was debating if I should go out there and get breakfast, or to just wait until he goes to his room and then I could make myself some breakfast. I decided with the second option. I started to sing Halo by Beyoncé until I heard a knock on my door. I groaned, Kyle's really annoying. He walked in with breakfast on a tray and a glass of apple juice. He set it on my nightstand and left without saying anything. I don't feel bad for being a bitch because he deserves it. He kidnapped me, yelled at me, called me names, and fucked me. Why wouldn't I be mad at him?

I sat in my bed just eating breakfast. Once I was finished, I brought everything to the kitchen and started cleaning. I saw Kyle on the couch working on his laptop. He looked up at me while I gazed at him. I looked away and continued doing the dishes. When I looked back at the couch, he was gone.

I heard a door close and lock. So now he's avoiding me? He has no right to be upset with me, should be upset with him. After I was done cleaning the dishes, I walked over to his office. Before I knocked, I could hear a faint sound of moaning, screaming, grunting, talking and a slapping sound. He's jacking off? I banged on the door and I heard the noise suddenly stop. A few seconds later the door was unlocked and opened. There stood a shocked and shirtless Kyle.

I can be mad all I want, but his body does something to me that makes me crave him.

"Hey." His voice was raspy. I don't know why I came over here. What was I supposed to be saying to him? I just stared at him, we looked in each other's eyes for what felt like ages. He cleared his throat. "Um. Can I help you?" He said softly.

Oh crap. My arms swung around his neck to lower him towards me and I stood on my tippy toes. I kissed him forcefully, and as if I had been starving for his touch. His hand went to my back and slid down until they were on my butt. He squeezed my butt and I could feel him starting to lift me up. I wrapped my legs around his hips and we kept kissing. He walked us into his room and closed the door. He laid me gently on the bed, and gazed at me. He just looked at me as if I was some sort of meal that he wanted to eat. I sat up and crossed my arms. I pouted at him and he groaned. He left the room and came back with a white box. He handed me my new iPod touch. It was gold and beautiful. I turned it on and found out that he had already set it up for me.

"Thanks." I was about to walk out of his room until he grabbed me and picked me up. He walked over to his bed and sat down. Then placed me on his lap. I could feel his erection on my butt, which surprisingly didn't bother me, it kinda turned me on. He held on strongly to me as I tried to pry his arms off of me. Just because I kissed him, doesn't mean I forgave him. It just means that we still like each other.

"Just sit with me Ashley."

"No. And don't you have to go work or something?"

"I'm going in tomorrow. But I want you to just sit with me." I sighed and decided to just give up fighting for right now. I turned on my iPod and started downloading games for me to play. I also downloaded Netflix and YouTube so that I could watch something if I was ever extremely bored. We sat there. It was somewhat relaxing and somewhat tense. I don't know how to explain it.

"Is there something else bothering you?" He whispered in my ear. I jumped a little because he broke the silence so close to my ear. I shrugged my shoulders. "Baby girl, you need to tell me so I could fix it."

I sighed, he was right. "Remember when we were at IHOP and you told Chase about what happened over the trip? Well I didn't appreciate that. No, I hated that you thought you could just tell people what we do intimately. Like, it's none of their business and it was supposed to remain in between us. You didn't even ask if you could tell him. You just went ahead and did it."

"Next time, I'll ask you if it's okay, or I just won't tell them. Alright Princess?" I nodded.

"Wait, what do you mean by next time?"

"I scheduled you a doctors visit. Let's go before we're late." I got off his lap.

"You didn't answer my question and why do I need to go to the doctors?"

"I'll tell you in the car. Go get dressed." I rushed out of his room and into mine. I walked into the closet and picked an outfit. I decided to go with a black halter neck romper with tassles around the leg holes and my white converse. I didn't put a bra or panties on, because I felt like being free today. I grabbed my iPod and the charger and headed towards the door where Kyle was waiting for me. He grabbed my hand and we left the penthouse. We took his convertible and left. We were at the doctor's office in about 15 minutes and we were helped soon after.

"So you must be Miss Rowens, am I correct?" The female doctor asked me.

"Yes."

"And you're here to take a pregnancy test and to get on birth control?" I was shocked that I was here for that. I looked at Kyle who was in the room with me.

"Yeah, she needs both of those."

"Who are you sir?"

"I'm her boyfriend." She nodded. She took out a box from her pocket in her lab coat and handed it to me.

"So I'm going to take you to the bathroom and I need you to pee on the stick and then bring it back, so we can check the results." I nodded. I hopped off the patient table and followed her to the bathroom while Kyle waited in the room. It was easy for me to pee, because I drank apple juice this morning. I brought the stick back to the women in a paper towel and she grabbed it. She set it aside while she asked me about my sex life and to make sure that I would need birth control pills. She wrote my prescription and told us where we could pick it up.

"Are you ready for the results of your test?" I nodded my head. Kinda scared that I could be pregnant. Kyle looked up at the woman with a cautious face,

"You're not pregnant!" I smiled and thanked God. Because I was definitely not ready to be a mother. We left the doctors office and went to pick up my prescription from CVS. The woman behind the desk told me that I had to wait 7 day after taking birth control consistently before having unprotected sex. Kyle was happier than I was.

"Let's go out."

"Like a date?"

"Ew no. Why would I want to go on a date with you?" He laughed. I stopped walking and felt disrespected. Any guy would be lucky to go on a date with me. "Princess, I'm just kidding. I would love to go out with you."

"Wait what?"

"I need to tell my bffs that the hottest girl in the world just asked me out." He fluttered his eyelashes. I started laughing hysterically.

"Wow. You think I'm the hottest girl in the world?" I joked with him.

He slid into his car. "Uhh. Did I say that?" He chuckled and blushed, I thought it was cute.

"Yup." I got in and we left. While we were driving, he put his hand onto my thigh and left it there. It sent tingles throughout my body and it was a welcomed feeling. I couldn't help but think that I am so lucky that I didn't end up pregnant.

(A/N) so Ashley is just like me, I ignore people when I'm mad at them.... like my neighbor that I told you guys about. He's a low key photographer and everyone at my school pays him to take their pictures. I never pay him, but he does it anyway. So we were supposed to go to this abandoned golf course near our house so he can take pictures and he ditched me. He went to some girl's house to get head. Like... so I told him that he was cut and he wanted to know why so I told him. He said "You said you didn't want to give me head or fuck, so I asked a thot to do it." First that's nasty, second we planned to go to the golf course two days ahead. Now that I'm ignoring him, he keeps trying to come up to me, but I avoid him. But yeah... I'll keep you updated.

Thank you for reading, commenting and voting (if you're loyal). If not... just enjoy, loyal people enjoy also.

Peace from the East. (I live on the east coast.)

(26) Problems

Kyle's POV

It has been a week since I brought Ashley to the doctors to get on the pill. I'm honestly excited to fuck her once again tonight. As I sit inside of Victoria's Secret waiting for her to try everything on, I'm just thinking about undressing her. Sometimes she came out and asked if I liked what she had on, other times she wouldn't. It's been a nice experience dating her. I mean, I don't ever date because most women are money hungry whores, sluts or they'll end up getting hurt in the long run. That's one of my concerns with Ashley. I don't ever want her to be sad or ever get hurt, so I'm always with her, which has impacted my work. I haven't been able to spend as much time at the club, or if I did, I would bring Ashley with me. She got along with a few of the women who worked there.

"I'm done. We can go now." She kissed me and grabbed my hand. We walked to the register and purchased the stuff. As we walked out of the store I realized that there was a man watching us very carefully. I thought it might just be some creep. We visited a few more stores and this unknown man was following us. I knew we would be safe because it was just one man and I could easily take him, or his life. I brought Stanley, the name for my favorite gun. Ashley walked into Forever 21 and I figured that this would be the perfect time to confront this stalker. I walked up to him and still couldn't recognize him.

"Hey dude, are you following us?" He smirked and chuckled.

"Alejandro wants his drugs back and soon. Or else there will be hell to pay." I took this as a threat and punched the guy in the gut. He hunched over and I leaned down towards him.

"Tell that son of a bitch to go fuck himself, and he's not getting anything." I said angrily to this punk. I was about to walk to go find Ashley, until the punk opened his mouth again.

"He knew you would try something like this." I turned around abruptly.

"What?" I asked, I was really pissed.

"He knew you would do something like this. He thought he would get a compensation until you return his shit." I heard a fight break out near the back of the store and a scream. The guy chuckled. "Ah. Looks like he got it. He wants his drugs within the next 2 weeks or else the girl gets it." My eyes went wide when I realized what he was talking about. Ashley. I ran to the back of the store to see what happened and to get my girl back. By the time I got there, it was too late. She wasn't there, only the bags full of her clothes laid on the ground. I cursed loudly and pulled out my phone. I called Sam and told him to arrange a meeting with everyone because we had a crisis. I ran out the store and rushed out the mall. I drove quickly down the highway to the club. Once I got there, I was pleased that everyone was in the conference room. They all stood up and looked at me to hear the reason as to why this meeting was called.

"ASHLEY HAS BEEN KIDNAPPED BY ALEJANDRO." I yelled out loud. Everyone was shocked and angry. "We need to get her back."

"What did he say he wanted?" Alonzo asked.

"The drugs we stole."

"We sold them, we can't get it back." Clyde said.

"DO I LOOK LIKE I'M STUPID? I KNOW WE SOLD THEM." I yelled, I was really pissed and stressed out. They better not put a hand on my baby girl. I started pacing around the room and everyone was staring at me.

"Let's come up with a plan to get rid of Alejandro and get Ashley back."

I stopped pacing. "Yeah, no duh. That son of a bitch shouldn't be living after the stunt he pulled."

"We could have someone be a double agent and pretend to work for him, but really be working for us."

"Okay. Does anyone else have any ideas?" I raised my voice. Many people shook their heads or tried to think.

"We have to find out where his hideout is and where he is keeping Ashley. I suggest that we start by finding Ashley and then killing him." I heard someone say.

"And how do you expect us to do that?" I asked.

"Well we could have someone get close to him and find out secrets."

"THAT WILL TAKE TOO FUCKING LONG." I yelled out becoming pissed. I can't believe that no one has came up with a good answer yet.

"I'll call my father, he should have an idea of what to do." Alonzo left the room while dialing his father. A few minutes later Alonzo came back inside and told us that his father was on his way.

Maybe now we'll actually get a good enough plan sorted out and start on it as soon as possible.

The door opened quickly and there stood an angry looking Italian man.

He walked towards the head of the table and everyone watched him including me. I hope to be as powerful as him one day and to make many people fear me.

"Hello gentlemen. Are you just gonna stare or are we going to get shit done?" He raised his voice at everyone. "Hello Kyle." He shook my hand, then his son's. We filled him in on what happened and he listened intently.

"First, we have to find out where he is. Because when we find him, we'll find your little giocattolo." Some of the Italian men smiled, I had no idea what he called my baby girl, for his sake, I never will.

I nodded in agreement and he started with a plan. He said he knows people that are quite close to Alejandro and that we could start from there. I glanced at my watch and it was 8:00 pm. Fuck.

"Everyone, you're excused. Go home and get some rest because tomorrow, we are gonna be busy." Everyone left except for Alejandro, his father and I.

"Maybe you should just let her go. People told me that you were with her just to fuck her. She's just a fuck toy. She doesn't mean anything to you." What Alonzo just said had pissed the fuck out of me. I punched him in the jaw and he took a few steps back because he had lost his balance. He looked up at me and I saw anger in his eyes.

"DON'T. EVER. SPEAK OF ASHLEY LIKE THAT AGAIN." I spit harshly. Alonzo's father just watched. I stormed out of the club and drove home. I don't know why I was in a rush, it's not like anyone is at home waiting for me. Anymore.

_____(A/N) sorry this chapter is so short. I promise the next one will be longer.

I hope y'all like the book so far and keep reading, commenting and voting. Thank you!!

Abrazos y besos!

(27) Where Am I?

☐ ☐TRIGGER WARNING!! If you can't bare the thought of rape or any violence, then this chapter and a few after it might trigger you. Beware.

Ashley's POV

I woke up inside a dark room. The walls were cement and there was only one door, no windows at all. In this room, there was a ugly looking cot, a small table and a suitcase. I was sitting on the small cot, which was really uncomfortable. I don't know where I am or what time it is and to be honest, I'm really scared. I got up from the couch and walked towards the suitcase. I was so close but my ankle was restrained, it was tied to the ugly little cot, so I was unable to go to far. I got back on the cot and pulled the blanket over me. I thought about screaming for help, but I didn't want the people that kidnapped me to know I was awake before I advised a plan to get out. I looked up towards that ceiling and spotted a small black camera. Then another one in another corner. Both were pointed towards this cot.

A few moments later the door opened. In walked a man. He wasn't ugly, but it would be bad for me to say as a taken girl, that this man was hot. He had black hair and black stubble on his face. His muscles bulged through his shirt as he crossed his arms and he was about 6 feet 4 inches.

"Hola chica." The man spoke in Spanish. Thank God I took advanced level Spanish.

"Hola. ¿Dónde estoy?" The man looked surprised that I knew Spanish. He smirked and then walked a little closer to me. I scooted back on the cot until my back was pushed up against the wall.

"Well, you are in my dungeon." His accent was pretty strong, but I was still able to understand him.

"Why? Why am I here?"

"Tus novio, owes me drugs. He stole drugs from me, so I stole something precious from him."

"He wouldn't do that. He doesn't do drugs." The man chuckled then sat on the cot.

"You are precious." He touched my cheek and I flinched. "But you are very stupid. Your boyfriend stole my drugs to sell them and make money. I want my drugs back, or I want the money that he made." He said angrily.

"What if he doesn't give you anything. What, what'll happen to me?"

"Well, you see those cameras?" He pointed to the cameras. "We aren't going to hurt you all the time, just sometimes, then we send the videos to tus novio." I got scared, what does he mean by hurt me. I started shaking, scared for my life.

"I don't mean anything to him. He's going to let it happen. He doesn't care."

"I think differently chica. One of my sources told me that he had a meeting last night, to figure out how to rescue you and kill me." Is it true? Is Kyle really going to try and save me?

My stomach growled and he smiled. "¿Te quieres desayuno?" I nodded my head. Breakfast sounds so good right now. The man got up, but before he left I asked him a question.

"¿Cuál es tu nombre?" He smiled.

"Alejandro."

I sat there. Thinking. Alejandro. His name is Alejandro. I can't believe I was kidnapped because I'm in a relationship with Kyle. It doesn't make sense, why take me, when you could just take him. I know it's wrong to think that way, but it honestly didn't make any sense to me. I wonder how they are going to hurt me. Like on Wattpad, they cut people and torture them, they cut off limbs. They better not cut off my fingers or toes. I hope they don't try to force me to do any intimate acts because I'd rather die. I mean it, I don't understand how people do it, but I congratulate survivors for being strong.

The door opened again and I smelt delicious food. Alejandro was carrying a tray with food and a cup of orange juice. He smiled. I stood up and started slowly walking towards him.

"Stop. He commanded." I stopped with a confused look on my face. "If you want desayuno, get naked." He smirked. A shiver ran down my spine in disgust. How could he. And why would I get naked, I mean, yes I am hungry. But, I'm not desperate.

"No." I said bravely. I didn't know how long it had been since I ate my last meal. I was starving, but I'm not getting naked for another man. Alejandro shrugged his shoulders and turned to walk out the door. But my stomach was hurting badly of hunger. "Wait." I called out. He turned around and walked towards me. He set he food onto the table and stood back to watch me get undressed. I took off my crop top, then my shorts. I kinda just stood there as he ogled at my body.

"Keep going, bonita." I slowly reached behind me and unclasped my bra. I slid the straps down my arms and took my bra off. Alejandro licked his lips and I felt defiled. I hooked my thumbs in my underwear band and slid them off. I covered my parts and sat on the cot. Alejandro picked up my clothes and left. I pulled the small table towards me, and started eating my somewhat warm food. There were 2 pancakes, 3 pieces of bacon and some scrambled eggs. I ate my food hurriedly and gulped down my orange juice. My stomach felt full and less pained than it did earlier. Everything came crashing back to me. I was kidnapped, the man who kidnapped me made me undress for him, and now I'm locked in a horrible cement room. I bawled my eyes out. The tears came down like a waterfall that would never stop flowing.

I can't believe I'm thinking this but, the first time I got kidnapped was a lot better than this time. The door opened and in walked some other guy. He stared at me crying and smirked. I grabbed the blanket and wrapped myself in it. I sat there crying and thinking about how much I missed my old life. I miss Taylor, my mom, my dad and my little brother. Ugh, my brother always told me to stop calling him my little brother since he was a lot taller than me. I chuckled. I wiped the tears away and laid down. I drifted off to sleep, but not before I prayed to God hoping that someone would rescue me.

•••

Kyle's POV

"Okay, okay." The guy pleaded. Victor had just put the second blade in this guys leg.

"Come on Antonio. We don't have all day." I stepped closer to him and crossed my arms. The guy was tied to a chair in his living room. This is the 5th guy in the past 6 hours that my gang has had to torture. None of them knew anything about this plan that Alejandro had. I was hoping that this guy would. "WHERE THE FUCK IS ALEJANDRO." I yelled harshly. The guy winced and looked scared.

"All I know is that he said he was going to take her to the 'dark'." The guy said. I looked over to Victor to see if he knew anything about this so called 'dark'. Victor shook his head.

"What and where the fuck is the dark?" I said harshly. The man shook his head, so I took a few steps back and Victor went back up to him.

"Let's start with the thumb. Since you need it the most." Victor said with a sadistic smile. He got a Dremel with a small rotary saw piece. He powered it on and grabbed the man's thumb. Victor started cutting the man's thumb and the man screamed loudly. Victor stopped before he reached the bone. "Wanna tell us about the 'dark' or do you want me to continue?"

"Ple..please..please stop. Okay, um. The 'dark' is where Alejandro takes the women that he captures and where he usually punishes them, along with some friends."

"What do you mean by 'punish'." I asked. I was starting to worry about Ashley.

"So in your case, he would ask for something in a specific amount of time. If you don't deliver, he'll send you a video of himself raping the woman or in some cases his friends raping her. He calls it the 'dark', not because it's dark in their, but because the people in their take punishing to the sexual extreme. Like hardcore BDSM and stuff. They have a huge room with all sorts of devices. It's horrible. They don't hurt the woman's body too badly. They ruin her mind."

It sounded horrible. I didn't want Ashley to have to go through something like that. I felt a tug in my chest. If he hurts my baby girl, then I'll find his family and kill them. I'll torture them myself and kill them. He's gonna regret laying a finger on my Ashley.

"Where can I find this 'dark'?" I asked. He shrugged his shoulders. Victor walked closer to Antonio with the Dremel in his hand.

"I'm serious, I honestly don't know. I'll tell you something else just dont cut off my thumb please." The man said, he was shaking because he was scared that he wasn't going to have a thumb on his right hand. I listened. "Alejandro said that someone that is currently working for you is really spying on you. He said that you always had him near. That's it."

"WHAT"S HIS NAME? WHO'S SPYING ON ME?" I yelled. The man shrugged his shoulders and was shaking a lot more violently.

I sighed. "Victor, take out the blades and give him the speech." I left Antonio's house and got into the truck. I called Alonzo.

"Any luck with Antonio?"

"Yeah. He told me that she's being held in a place called the 'dark'."

"Oh shit. I've heard of that place. I might know someone who knows where it is located. Is that all you got from Antonio?"

"He also said that someone is double-crossing me, and that I always had him near."

"Call in a meeting. I'll try to figure out this traitor." I hung up and Victor got into the car.

"So what's next Boss?"

"We're calling in a meeting." I texted Sam to tell everyone to go back to the club because it's urgent.

(A/N) not as long as I wanted it to be, but that's ok. It was over 500 words more than the last chapter, so I kept my promise. And if you don't know Spanish, then educate yourself. I tried to make it as easy as possible to understand what was happening.

But I honestly can't believe that Alejandro is that ruthless. Ugh.. people like him in real life should jump off a cliff. Anyway... how'd you guys like it???

Don't forget to comment, vote, share, whatever it is you do. Ciao for now

(28) The Mole

▢Trigger Warning!

Kyle's POV

I walked into the conference room and to say I was angry as fuck was an understatement. I slammed the door and everyone looked scared.

"Alonzo and I are going to be interviewing each of you, one by one. No one is allowed to leave, so call your wives or girlfriends, and tell them you're not going to make it for dinner." Many people looked confused or picked up the phone to call someone. I looked around to see if anyone looked suspicious. I couldn't tell who the mole was, but when I find out who it is, he's going to wish he was never born.

I walked into my office with Alonzo and we devised a plan on how we were going to interview them. "I suggest you start with that secretary guy you work with. The guy did say that the mole was close to you and or Ashley." I nodded. "Who else did you have around Ashley or yourself a lot?"

"Um... Chase, Wesley and Ricardo." Alonzo nodded his head. He got up from his chair and went to get Sam.

"Sam sit down." I ordered. He looked nervous, especially when Alonzo closed the door. This kid couldn't have been the mole. He's like 19 and looks so innocent.

"Sir, what am I here for?" He asked nervously.

"Well we have a mole." Sam gasped. I raised an eyebrow. "The guy that we spoke to earlier said that this person is close to me, and your the closest person to me. You know my schedule, my plans, where I'm at or where I'm going to be, you know the people in my life and so on." Sam nodded slowly.

"Sir, you can't possibly think that I'm the mole." He sounded insulted.

"We are just gathering information. So, would you take a bullet for Kyle?" Alonzo asked.

"Yes."

"And how did you feel about him stealing Alejandro's drugs. How do you feel about his relationship with Ashley?"

"I mean... Stealing drugs from Alejandro got him into this mess, but it was a good move on Kyle's part. Alejandro had been trying to take our customers and turf. So, I thought showing some power was a great move. On another note. Kyle's relationship with Ashley is none of my business. I mean, she has had a great effect on him. He's a lot nicer now, and is a little more patient and relaxed. So, I encourage their relationship, she's a good match for him." Alonzo and I nodded. We both took a few notes on his answer and dismissed him. We had to tell him to go to the private rooms instead of the conference room because we didn't want the mole to escape.

We interviewed Chase and Ricardo next. I would've thought that Chase was the mole because he was jealous that I had Ashley and he had nothing. That could cause someone to be disloyal, but surprisingly that wasn't the case. He got angry at whoever the mole was and was already angry that Ashley had been taken. Ricardo passed with flying colors.

Next was Wesley. He walked in and sat down. He looked somewhat nervous. "So Boss, what's going on?" He asked. Alonzo came in after him and sat down. Wesley's leg kept moving up and down quickly as if he was trying to keep his composure. I looked at Alonzo and Alonzo nodded his head to signal that he was thinking the same thing.

"Earlier today, someone told us that we had a mole. Someone that works for Alejandro told us that he was close to me or Ashley." Wesley started looking around nervously.

"We just want to know if you knew who the mole was, or if you are the mole." Alonzo said. Wesley's eyes went wide.

"No." He cleared his throat. "No, I'm not the mole. Why would it be me?"

"Because you work closely with me, and you've seen how I act around Ashley, so you would know that she means a lot to me."

"Sorry, but you got the wrong guy." Wesley started to stand up.

Alonzo pushed him back onto the chair. "We're not finished with you. To me, it seems that you are in a rush to leave this interrogation as if you are guilty. You were going to go and call Alejandro and tell him that we know that you are the mole. Weren't you? So, why'd you spy on Kyle and why did you let Alejandro take Ashley?" Alonzo shouted at Wesley.

****

Wesley's POV

Alonzo yelling at me made me pissed off, and scared. I know, what kind of mole gets scared when someone yells at them? Me, I do. Tears started rolling down my eyes when I looked at Kyle to see him beyond pissed and he looked like he wanted to end my life. I might as well come clean now.

"You wanna know why I did it? I did it because one day, Alejandro was at my house about to torture me for your address. But, I didn't give it to him, no. I offered him something better. I told him I would be the mole, and I would be his way in. He happily agreed and paid me for it. When I found out that you were dating someone it made me mad." I spat. Kyle had a confused look on his face. "Yeah, that's right. I had a crush on you. A big one. I thought that if I was able to be Ashley's bodyguard I could easily let her run away and be there to comfort you. Then maybe you would fuck me or become my boyfriend or something. But no, all I heard was giggles and yelling when you guys were together. It made me so mad to see that she won you over. So, I told Alejandro and he waited until the perfect time to kidnap her. I thought that if she was kidnapped, then you would be so sad, that you would fuck anything with a heartbeat. Like me. But I guess not." I finally finished. I knew my face was a mess. I probably had snot running out my nose and tears all over my face.

Alonzo and Kyle looked at each other, shocked. I wiped my face with my shirt. I saw Kyle and Alonzo talking.

Alonzo walked out and a few moments later, Victor, Chase and a few others came into the office.

"Guys, we had a mole and I found out who it is. The reason he did it..." Kyle looked at me and I shook my head, hoping he wouldn't tell them my secret.

"He did it because he wanted more money. So he started working for Alejandro." Alonzo said.

"Guys, drug him and bring him to the 'garage'." Kyle said. A few of them grabbed me, while one went to get the chloroform. I started thrashing in their grips, not wanting to go to the 'garage'.

The 'garage' was a place where Kyle took people to torture them. He would torture them until he got answers, or until he wasn't angry or for revenge. Soon a cloth was placed over my mouth and nose and I tried to hold my breath. It didn't work, soon I started seeing black dots until all I saw was black.

****

Ashley's POV

"3 more days. If he doesn't pay up, I'll have to record myself hurting you." Alejandro said, while he sat next to me on the cot. He tried to sound sad about the idea of hurting me, but his twisted smile was saying otherwise.

"You don't have to hurt me though. You could let me go and I won't tell a single soul." I tried to plead with him. He shook his head.

"No, but we do have to give him a reminder to give us our merchandise back." He stood up and started walking to the large briefcase. I was actually scared. Is he going to cut off my fingers or something? Because I would rather him to go fuck himself or jump off a cliff.

He put the briefcase on the small table and unlocked it using a code. Once it opened, I was able to see what was inside of it. There were a bunch of sex toys.

"Ashley, do you need to pee?" Alejandro said with his back towards me.

"No." I said quietly. I was so scared for what was about to happen. He turned around and had a set of handcuffs.

"Stand up and turn around Ashley." I shook my head. I scooted closer to the wall, as if that would do anything. He reached over and yanked my arm towards himself. I stood up and felt the tears running down my face.

"We have barely begun. No need for tears chica." He grabbed my wrists and forced them behind me. He put on the handcuffs, so I was unable to fight back with my hands. He pushed me back onto the cot and I fell forwards. My butt was sticking up in the air while my chest was on the bed. "Wow. Tú tienes una bonita culo." He slapped my butt and I winced. I felt his finger tracing my butt hole.

"Please don't. Nothing has ever went up there." I begged him. All of a sudden I felt his finger forcing its way up my butt. I tried tightening my butt, but being bent over and doing that was really hard. I started to cry harder.

"You are very tight, chica." He pulled his finger out and this time, he inserted two fingers. He went slowly, but it hurt like a bitch. I screamed and I heard him laugh. He then started moving his fingers in and out of my butt. The friction that was being caused, made it hurt even more as he pushed his fingers in and out of me. I felt and heard him spit. He had successfully made it land where his finger assault was happening. The saliva helped a little bit.

He pulled his fingers out and I though he was done. I was unable to see him, but I heard this moving around in his briefcase. I felt something cold touch me. "This is called a butt plug. It might hurt a little. I'll be back a little later to take it out. But I need you to relax so I could push it in. It'll be less painful that way." I didn't know what to do. Should I relax, so this will end sooner, or should I continue to fight back?

I'll go with the first option. I tried my best to relax. I took a deep breath and he started pushing the butt plug into my butt. I'm pretty sure it had lube on it, because it was able to slide into me. It still hurt, but it was less painful than I thought. Once it was done, Alejandro pulled me up.

He stared into my eyes and saw how sad and hurt I looked. The height difference was big, but not as big as Kyle and I's. Alejandro pulled me into his body and started leaning towards my face. One of his hands were squeezing my butt, while the other one was on the back of my neck. He pulled my face closer to his, while I tried going in the opposite direction. He forcefully kissed me, he tried to slide his tongue into my mouth, but I wouldn't let him. He backed away and smiled.

"We are going to work on that kiss of yours." He winked and closed the briefcase. He put the briefcase on the other side of the room and left. My wrists were still in hand cuffs and I was still crying. I was so disgusted in him. I spit onto the floor, trying to get the nasty taste of him off my lips. I sat down on the cot. Now that he's gone, I could try to get out of the handcuffs. Thank God I'm flexible. I slid my arms down my legs and was able to get my hands from behind me to in front of me. I laid down on the cot and pulled the covers on top of my body. I started to sob uncontrollably. I was molested. He touched me inappropriately and without my consent. I was about to drift to sleep, until I felt a buzzing. It scared me at first. It was a light vibration coming from my butt. Oh shit, this thing vibrates. The vibrations got more intense and I knew for a fact that this was Alejandro's doing. I stuck up the middle finger to the camera.

I thought about pulling the plug out of my butt, except I was scared of the punishment that would follow if I did. I was starting to feel aroused, but it was unwanted at this moment. If it were Kyle making me feel this way, then I would be so happy. But it wasn't Kyle, it was this twisted son of a bitch named Alejandro.

The vibrations must've been on high, because it was making me more aroused. I tried to hold in my moans, but it wasn't working. One escaped my mouth and as soon as it did, the door opened. It scared the living Jesus out of me. I jumped. I wasn't as horny now, but this vibrator inside of the butt plug was making me more aroused. I was unable to sleep and arousal was clouding my judgement. Alejandro walked up to my cot. He took the handcuffs off of me with some keys.

"Put your hands behind your back." He commanded. I followed his orders and he handcuffed me again. He pushed me onto the cot with my ass in the air.

WHACK What the fuck? That hurt like a bitch. He hit me with some type of paddle or something on my butt cheeks.*WHACK**WHACK*

"Don't ever move your hands again. Do you understand?" He hit me again

"Yes." I heard the paddle drop to the floor.

"Do you want me to help you cum?" I bit my lip. No, I didn't want him to touch me, but I'm so horny. I really needed some release. "Did you hear me? DO YOU WANT ME TO HELP?" He raised his voice.

"Yes." I whispered.

"Beg for it."

"Please help me cum. Please. Please help me release." I begged. I closed my eyes. I couldn't believe that I just said that. I felt his fingers start to touch my pûssy and it sent shock waves through me. It wasn't enough.

Then I felt 2 of his fingers enter my hole. He started finger fucking me. I was a moaning mess and I was screaming and I was pushing my ass towards his finger. I was desperate for release.

"I'M CUMMING!" I screamed out. I felt the strong ripples of pleasure wash over my body. He took his fingers out and I fell on my side as I continued my orgasm. As it subdued, I laid there trying to catch my breath.

"By the way. You taste magnificent." He walked towards the door then turned around. "Dinner will be down shortly." He left.

I started crying. I can't believe I just let him do that to me. I was so disgusted with myself. How could I let such a vulgar man touch me. He kidnapped me for God's sake. Soon the door opened and in came the bathroom man. He usually takes me to the bathroom so that I could freshen up. He unlocked my ankle, then my wrists.

"Bend over." I listened and did what he asked me to do. I felt him tug on the butt plug, so I helped by pushing outwards. It came out with a pop. He walked me to the restroom. Once I was there, he locked me inside and left me alone. I took a shower, used the bathroom and washed my hair. I knocked on the door to signal that I was finished. The bathroom man walked me back to the cement room and locked my ankle back to the cot. A few minutes later, Alejandro came in with my dinner.

"Hola chica. ¿Cómo estás?" He asked with a smile.

"I'm..." I didn't know how to answer. People usually say fine, even though they aren't fine. But I'm not one of those people. "Tired. Sad. Scared. I miss my family, friends and my boyfriend. Even though I shouldn't miss him because he's the reason I'm in this mess." I sighed. I stared at my food. Today I had a delicious looking cheeseburger and french fries.

"Well, once tus novio gives me my stuff, I'll let you go." He left. I sat there and ate my dinner. I imagined the beach that my family goes to every year. How we eat ice cream on the boardwalk or how we play Frisbee on the sand. I saw that on a TV show. You're supposed to imagine doing things when you're locked up. Imagining doing things in the real world is supposed to prevent you from going insane. I'm not too sure if it's working though.

(A/N) I woke up this morning and saw a very new very notification from @PolinEll so I wanted to give her a huge thanks. And also she voted for all my chapters thus far and I was so happy.

Go follow her. @PolinEll

Thank you everyone for reading. Don't forget to comment, vote and keep reading.

See ya later alligator!!

(29) Torture

Wesley's POV

I woke up in a dungeon. Oh yeah, they found out. Everything came swarming back to my mind. Like how I told Kyle that I have a huge crush on him. The door opened and there was Chase.

"THE BASTARD IS AWAKE!" He yelled out to the others. Chase walked in and punched me in the jaw. My face had a pounding in it from where he hit me. Before he could take another swing, Kyle stopped him. Kyle was shirtless and let me tell you, he has the body of a God. I would love to lick his abs.

I could feel myself starting to get hard, just thinking about him bending me over and fucking me. I licked my lips as I ogled his body. Then to interrupt it, Alonzo cleared his throat and I became angry.

Kyle pulled out a gun and shot me in the foot. I yelled out loud from the pain.

"That one was for being a traitor. And this one.." He shot me in the same foot. "Is for letting them take Ashley." Chase pulled out a gun and did the same thing to my other foot.

I looked down and my feet were surrounded by blood.

"Where is 'the dark'?" Kyle asked me all seriously. I would love for him to hate fuck me. Even though he shot me in the foot, I could forgive him.

"I don't know what you're talking about." I said, when in fact, I knew where it was and how to get inside. Kyle walked up to me and punched me twice. I spit some blood out of my mouth.

"Where is 'the dark'?" Alonzo yelled at me. I was scared, but I wasn't going to give it up. Why would I tell them where the 'dark' is at? So Kyle could have the person he loves while I can't? Nope, that's definitely not happening. Kyle whistled and in came Victor.

Shit. I knew Victor was good at this stuff. Now he's going to torture me. He set his bag on the ground and opened it.

"Hmm. What should we start with? The knives or the hammer?" He looked up at me while holding the objects.

"Excuse for one second." Alonzo left as he picked up the phone. I looked back at Kyle. Pleading with my eyes that he'll stop this, but I was met with anger and hatred.

"I'll go with the knives." Victor stood up with 5 or so knives in his hand and came towards me. He quickly stuck one in one leg and slowly stabbed another knife in the other leg. The pain was overwhelming and all I could do was scream.

Alonzo walked back in. "My father gave me the location of 'the dark'."

Kyle sighed and left. "I guess I'll have to finish this later." Victor said to me as he pulled the knives out. He left, then a doctor came in to sew my wounds.

****

Kyle's POV

I drove to the club, where we were going to devise a plan on how to get Ashley back and kill Alejandro. Once I arrived at the club, people were going crazy. I yelled at them, I told them to meet me in the conference room.

Once everyone was in there, I wanted to know why it was hectic.

"Why was everyone going completely crazy out there?"

"Alejandro sent a DVD."

"He left it at the back door." I was surprised. But also worried.

"Where's it now?"

"In the TV sir." I turned on the TV and started the disk.

"Hello Kyle. You are probably trying to figure out where your precious little toy is right now, well let me tell you that she is safe. It's been 4 days since I have kidnapped her and you have 3 days until she gets severely hurt. Here's a little reminder, if you are planning anything else." ~ Alejandro

The disk then played a video from what looked like Ashley's dungeon. She was first made to strip for food. Then a second video showed of her being handcuffed and pushed onto a small bed. His fingers violated Ashley while she cried and screamed. I felt a tugging at my heart. I felt like crying and yelling and killing someone. Then I saw him stick a butt plug into her. No. I was supposed to be the first thing that went up there. He's gonna pay. He pulled her up and forcefully kissed her. She looked repulsed and sad. He put his nasty ass lips on my baby girl, I'm not just going to kill him. I'm going to torture him for days until he wishes that he was dead. The next clip was just her laying in bed crying. The one after that made me beyond pissed. His fingers were pleasuring her and she was moaning. He also hit her with a flogger. I can't believe this. I don't feel betrayed because sometimes your body gives into arousal, even if it's unwanted. When she came I was even angrier. I was supposed to be the only one that touched Ashley like that, I was supposed to be the only one that gave her release like that. Then when he tasted his fingers and commented on her sweetness while she cried, I lost my shit.

Another clip played. It must've been when Ashley had first gotten to 'the dark'. Alejandro was explaining to Ashley why she was there and what was going to happen to her.

"I don't mean anything to him. He's going to let it happen. He doesn't care."

I picked up a chair and threw it against the wall. Everyone was staring at me, but I didn't care. I only cared about getting back the girl that I love. Even though I've never told Ashley that I loved her, I do. But sadly she doesn't know that, sadly she thinks that I'm going to let her get hurt. She thinks I'm going to let her get hurt because I let her get kidnapped.

"I WANT TO KILL THAT BASTARD. WE ARE DOING THIS PLAN TOMORROW." Everyone nodded their heads. If I was angry, that meant all of them had to be angry too.

"Alonzo, where the fuck is this place?"

"It's in PG County. One of the guys that work there are best friends with my dad. He sent the post changes and the map of the place. He also said that he'll turn off the alarms, he just need to know the time." I nodded my head while Sam handed out the papers.

"Okay. We'll enter from the East and West side doors. They have 2 guards each, so that'll be easy to get through. Next we'll need both teams to split up. One half is going to the security room to kill those bitches, while the other half goes and kills the guards at the North door. We'll leave from the

North door, so we'll need a getaway driver. I need 5 people to come with me. Got it?" Everyone nodded their head.

"How many people are in the groups?"

"We'll have 10 people per group. So tell the others who couldn't make it. Make sure to send me who is in your group by 11 tonight." Everyone nodded and left.

"How'd you come up with a plan so fast?" Alonzo asked me on my way out.

"Video games and because I'm smart." I got in my car and went back to the 'garage'. I needed to relieve some anger. I know just who I'm gonna beat. I'll stop right before he could die, and leave him there clinging for his life.

(A/N) 2 chapters in one day?!?

Anyway, I hope you guys enjoyed this chapter. See you in the next one

(30) Mission: Ashley

Ashley's POV

I woke up in the morning feeling hungry, thirsty and with the need to use the restroom. I knocked on the door 3 times, signalling the bathroom man that I needed to use the bathroom. He opened the door and I was escorted to the bathroom. Once I was finished, he took me back to the cement room. I saw breakfast sitting on the small table waiting for me to eat it. Today there was a Belgium waffle and some bacon. I drizzled syrup onto my waffle and started eating. When I was about half way done, the door opened and in came Alejandro.

"¡Buenos dias, chica!" He sat down on the cot.

"Good morning." I responded nervously. He started playing with my hair.

"So, the man I sent to spy on Kyle hasn't called me back in a while. Do you know why bonita?" I swallowed my food and shook my head. He yanked my hair back causing me to lean backwards. "Because he misses you. He wants to find you. But that is not going to happen. You know why?" I shook my head again. "Say 'why'."

"Why?" I said in fear. He let go of his fist full of my hair and stood up.

"That's not going to happen because we are moving you to a different location at 8 tonight."

"Why are you telling me this?" I asked curiously and also because I was scared.

"Because, starting at 4 pm, I'm going to start hurting you. I just want you to know, that the torture will end at 8. When you have to leave." He smiled at me. I was scared for my life. Imagine someone saying that your torture was going to last for 4 hours. Yeah, scary right? I feel like pissing myself. But I remember my best friend always saying, "Mama ain't raise no bitch." I had to be a big girl and not back down.

I continued eating breakfast and Alejandro sorta just watched me eat, like a stalker. He left after a while and I continued to eat. I thought about what Alejandro said.

When I was done, a man came and grabbed my tray and dirty dishes. I laid down in my cot and went to sleep. I'm not lazy, there's just nothing I can do in here.

••*•*•*•*•*•*•*•*•*•*•*•*•*•*•*•

Kyle's POV

Alonzo, Jacob, Ricardo, Giovanni, and Nathan were with me waiting for this guy on the inside to text us. As soon as we got the go ahead, I told the squads on the East and West doors to go in and kill the security guards. We waited for 5 minutes when a message on the talkie said that we were clear to come in. We busted through the door and saw men lying on the ground, dead. We stepped over them, all of us had our weapons drawn, expecting the unexpected. We walked through the halls, opening every door that we saw. As I opened each one, the level of disappointment and fear rose. It was starting to feel unbearable, until I heard a loud scream. We all ran towards the scream, and there were already people from my side waiting at the door. The door was already opened and I was able to see Ashley.

I walked inside the small room with Alonzo beside me. We both were seething with anger as we held our guns pointed towards Alejandro. Alejandro had his arm wrapped around Ashley's neck and a gun pointed toward her head. He had a huge smile on his face while Ashley was crying. I hated the fact that everyone was seeing my baby girl naked. Her body is for me only. But, as much as I wanted to tell them to look away, I knew that they had to be ready to put a bullet through this guy.

"It's nice to finally meet you Kyle." He said sadistically.

"SHUT THE FUCK UP." I yelled. "GIVE ME BACK ASHLEY." Alejandro shook his head.

"Lo siento. That is not how it is going to work. Let me tell you what's going to happen. You are going to let me leave, and I'm going to take tu novia with me. If you try to shoot me, I will put a bullet through her pretty little head."

I looked at Alonzo. We both put our guns down. Ashley started to shake her head and cry more. "No, no, no. Please. Help me Kyle. Please, don't let him take me."

"I spokes to one of your friends and they told me what you would do in a situation like this. Prove it." A look of confusion went across Ashley's face. I had talked to Dylan about Taylor and making sure that Ashley's friend was okay. He had told me about how Ashley and Taylor talked about ways to get out of dangerous situations. I was impressed that Taylor shared that with Dylan. They must really like each other. Ashley's head lifted up and a smile was plastered on her face.

She let her body go limp, which was unexpected to Alejandro. She fell to the ground, then elbowed him really hard in the balls. When he crouched over to cup his most likely damaged balls, Ashley got up quickly and ran towards me. She jumped into my arms and kissed me. I felt her tears, and maybe mine too. I put her down, and looked at and angry Alejandro. He raised up his gun and was about to aim at Ashley, my stomach dropped. Just after I had gotten her back, she was about to be killed. In a split second, Alonzo shot Alejandro in the shoulder causing him to drop the gun. The men went up to Alejandro and put handcuffs on him. As they walked Alejandro out to the car, I grabbed the sheet off of the small bed and covered Ashley with it. I looked into her eyes and saw happiness and sadness. I hugged her, and I felt as if it was only her and I in the whole world.

I tucked my gun in my holster and picked Ashley up bridal style. "Close your eyes baby." I didn't want her to see a whole bunch of dead bodies on the ground. She was too innocent and she was broken. I didn't want to worsen the nightmares that I know are bound to come. I sat her in the back of the car and sat in the back with her. We looked at each other and it felt like the world was at a standstill. I knew it wasn't safe, but I needed her to be in my arms. I was going to protect her with my life from here on out. I pulled her onto my lap and hugged her. She leaned against my chest and sighed.

"You know I cried every night?" She said quietly. I felt bad for letting her out of my sight. I had been blaming myself everyday and every night. I kept telling myself that I was a horrible boyfriend who couldn't even keep his girlfriend safe. "I cried every night and everyday. All I did was lay on that small cot and think about my friends and family. I thought about my brother the most, which is pretty weird. We were always fighting, but we always had each other's back." I felt a tear go down my face. This was all my fault. For the rest of the ride, we were silent and enjoyed the company of the other person.

When we reached my building. I got out of the car and carried Ashley the whole way up. She's heavy, but it was worth it. She needs to know how much I value her. I brought her into my room and laid her in my bed. "Do you want to take a shower?" She nodded her head slowly. She got up and walked into my bathroom and shut the door. I don't know if that meant that she didn't want me in there or not. But, I was not going to let her out of my sight. I got some clothes from her room and laid them in my bed, I also grabbed her a clean towel. I walked into the bathroom and stripped. I walked into the shower and saw the most heartbreaking thing ever. Ashley was sitting on the floor inside the shower as the water came down, hitting her naked frame. She was bawling her eyes out and she looked so.... helpless. I turned off the shower and quickly grabbed her towel. I picked her up from the floor and wrapped her body in the towel. I sat down outside the shower, with her in my arms.

This is all my fault. I got her into this mess and I'm the one that made her fall for me. I shouldn't have fallen in love with her. I shouldn't have ever let my emotions get the best of me. Yet, I did. I don't regret choosing her, because it meant that she would be mine and mine only. It meant that I could be the reason she smiles and laughs. I let this beautiful woman cloud my judgement and this is what happened.

I rocked back and forth while rubbing her back. She held on tightly to the towel and cried.

I felt like she's been crying for hours when she had finally stopped. "Come on. We are taking a bath together." I stood up and she sat on the bathroom counter. I ran the bath water and added some bubble solution. I lit a few candles as the huge tub filled with water. Once the tub was filled to my liking, I shut the water off and got into the tub.

"Come here baby girl." I said softly. I held my arms out wide and signaled her to walk towards me with my hands. She slowly sat into the tub, on my lap. I held her in my embrace as she leaned against my body. I could still hear her sniffles, but I knew in this moment, that she would be okay. For now.

───────────────────────────

(A/N) this took a while idk why tho. This was an interesting chapter to write.

Hope y'all enjoyed this chapter and don't forget to vote, comment and keep on reading.

Duces.

(31) I'm Better

☐ ☐TRIGGER WARNING!! ALSO THIS CHAPTER CONTAINS A SEX SCENE!!PLEASE BE CAUTIOUS AND FOR MY YOUNGSTERS. YALL SHOULDN'T BE READING THIS STORY!!!

Kyle's POV

I woke up to crying. I glanced at the clock next to my bed and turned on my lamp. Ashley was crying in her sleep again which was difficult for me. It wasn't difficult because I was losing sleep, but because every time she cried, I was reminded that it was my fault. I shook her body, and she woke up frightened. She sat up and I quickly embraced her. She continued to cry as I tried my best to calm her down. I whispered sweet words in her ear until her crying turned into sniffles.

"Baby girl, you're okay now. You're safe with me." I whispered in her ear. She nodded softly and stayed in my embrace.

"It..it was hor-hor-horrible." She managed to say. I rubbed her back and kissed the top of her head. I rocked slightly hoping to calm her further. "It was painful. Especially when he stuck that thing... that thing inside of me."

"I know, I know." She scooted away from me and brought the blanket up to her chest. "How's therapy going so far?"

She shrugged. It's been two weeks since she's been back, and she's been going to therapy for a little over a week. I have a therapist come everyday to talk to her and sometimes the therapist would bring a survivor in with her. "I mean, we talk about what happened. It's hard and I cry a lot. But, the nightmares aren't as bad as they used to be. Right?"

"Yeah, you aren't screaming or trying to fight back." I looked at my ribs. She had punched me in my side really hard, which ended up leaving a bruise.

"Sorry about that." She had a small smile.

"Hey. It's good to know that I have a girlfriend that can punch." She chuckled and so did I. We stared into each other's eyes. Just looking for comfort and and to know that everything was surely going to be okay. I grabbed her hand and brought it up to my lips. I kissed her hand then pulled her closer. I kissed her softly on the lips and she kissed me back. I turned off the lamp and we laid back down, we spooned each other. Soon enough, we were both asleep.

••*•*•*• 3 months later *•*•*•*•*•*•*•

Ashley's POV

"Stop it." I yelled to Kyle as he chased me around the penthouse with whipped cream on his hand. He had caught me spraying the can of whipped cream into my mouth, which I'm not supposed to do. Now he's chasing me with it, trying to smear whip cream on my face. I was obviously not fast enough because he soon caught up and an arm snaked around my waist. He pulled me towards his body and wiped the cream all over my face. Him and I couldn't stop laughing.

"Got ya babe." He said. I smiled. Then an idea popped into my head. I pretended to be sad. I stuck out my bottom lip and crossed my arms. He looked at me as if he was guilty.

"I want a hug."

"Come to daddy then." He had a seductive smile on his face. I ran into his arms and wiped my face all on his bare chest. He took a deep breath and let go of me. "Oh no you didn't." I ran from him quickly. I ran into my room, but remembered there were no locks on my door. I hid in my closet, trying my best not to let anything touch my face. The door swung open and I started laughing uncontrollably. I stepped out of the closet.

"Oh babe, what happened to you? You have whipped cream all over yourself." I started to laugh again.

"Oh I wonder." He said sarcastically. He picked me up and tossed me over his shoulder.

"Put me down."

"No. I think we need to wash off because this whipped cream feels disgusting." He set me down once we entered his bathroom. I pulled his shirt that I was wearing off while he took off his pants. Once we were fully naked, he just gazed at me. I moved my arms, in order to cover my bits.

"Never hide your beauty away from me. You got that?" I nodded. I let my arms fall back to my sides and he lowered to kiss me. I gave him a peck and giggled. I walked to the shower and turned it on.

I'm so in love with this shower. It's one of those showers that has the water coming from the ceiling like rain. It also has those jets on the wall. Ugh, wonderful.

Once the water was hot, I stepped inside with Kyle right behind me. I stood under the stream of water and felt the droplets wash away the whipped cream. I started washing off my body with my wash cloth and soap. I rinsed off, and I was about to step out the shower until someone grabbed my wrist. I turned my head and looked at him smiling.

"I need some help." He glanced down at his cöck. I licked my lips and turned around fully. I wrapped my hand around his member and started stroking him slowly. We stared into each other's eyes. His were full of lust and I had no doubt that mine were too. He let out a groan, which told me that I was found a great job. I squatted and looked up at his face. He looked down at me with anticipation. I kissed the tip and licked the under side of his cöck. He turned off the water and I continued to tease him. I felt his hand move to the back of my head and trying to push my mouth onto his member. I complied and let him slide into my mouth. I heard him let out a groan. I started to bob my head slowly, until I was at the point of deep throating. His head tilted back and I knew that it meant he was going to cum soon. I closed my eyes and started to bob my head faster. I was choking on his cöck and my eyes were welled up with tears.

His hands moved under my arms and his body bent over. He pulled me up and looked into my eyes. I knew what he was asking. Luckily, I had been taking the pill. I gave him a reassuring nod. He picked me up and we kissed. His lips dominating mine, his tongue declared entrance and my mouth fell into submission. I allowed his tongue into my mouth, our tongues danced together until I felt the sheets of the bed against my back. He stood up, while I laid on the bed staring up at him.

He got down on his knees and spread my legs apart. He started kissing the inside of my thighs making me become wetter and wetter. The desperation for him was getting stronger and stronger as he teased me. He nibbled, licked and sucked the insides of my thighs and on my mound.

Finally his tongue gently flicked over my clît. I let out a moan that needed to be let out. I felt his fingers find my slît and start tracing the outside of it. His tongue started swiping my clît faster causing me to moan and squirm. My hand found his head and his hair. My hand entangled in his hair, pulled him closer to my core. I needed this release badly. It had been a while since I've been touched my someone that I actually like.

"Ohh fuck. Kyle." I moaned. I felt his lips move into a smile as he continued to lick my core.

His fingers pushed their way inside of me until his knuckle was against me. He started thrusting his fingers in and out of my slît, causing my back to arch off the bed and my toes to curl. I knew the edge was near as he continued to eat me out. His tongue lapped away at my core causing me a great amount of pleasure.

"KYLE! YESS! FUCK!" I screamed out loud. "I'm so close, I'm about to cum."

"C'mon baby girl. Let me see you cum." I heard him say seductively. Finally I felt myself gush.

I felt euphoria run through my body as I orgasmed. My body shook with pleasure and I felt so content. My eyes shuddered, then closed as the orgasm sent waves throughout my body. It was powerful and earth shattering.

After the orgasm subsided, I was finally able to continue with what we started. Kyle was standing up and watching me, his eyes were full of lust. "Get on your hands and knees." He demanded, and I submit to him. I felt him rubbing his hands in circles on my ass. All of a sudden the warmth was taken away, but not for long. I felt his hands slap my ass. I yelped. It stung a little.

"I love your ass baby girl." His hands started rubbing circles on my butt again, soothing the little pain that he caused. But, him slapping my butt also made me wetter.

One of his hands moved to my hip and the other was behind me. I felt the tip of his cöck rubbing my pûssy. He was teasing me once again. I pushed myself back in attempt for his length to enter me, but it was a fail. He chuckled.

"You want me badly baby girl? Tell me then." He continued to rub my pûssy, teasing me. No doubt that this was very hard for him, to resist fucking me right now.

"Kyle. Please fuck me. I need you, I need this." Once I moaned that, he thrusted hard into me.

I let out a scream once he finally put his length inside of me. He slid out, to the point where only the tip of his cock was inside of me. Then he slammed back into me, causing me to scream again. He started thrusting in and out of me with force causing me to scream and moan loudly. His nails were digging into my hips, the pain and pleasure mixed beautifully together. I pushed back as his slammed forward, meeting him halfway. His large hand found its way into my hair and he pulled on it. It lead to a yelp and then turning into a moan.

"Fuck baby! You're so tight." He grunted as he fucked me. "Turn over." I was confused until he pulled out and tried flipping me onto my back. Once I was on my back, he slid into me. I let out a moan. The feeling of his cöck filling me up, was like when you finally eat after being hungry for a long time. He started fucking me, my legs wrapped around his waist as he pounded me. His hand made its way to my neck and he started choking me. He didn't choke me hard, just enough to make the sensations in my lower region intensify.

We stared into each other's eyes as he fucked me, making this more intimate and passionate. He quickly swooped down to my face and his lips were on mine. He continues moving his member inside of me and the feeling was becoming too much. He started kissing on my jaw and neck. My hands found their way into his hair, as he left hickies along my neck. My back arched off the bed and my toes began to curl. His hand slithered down between our bodies and found my clît. He started rubbing me fast. I was approaching my climax and so was he. He started thrusting in and out of me faster. I moaned and screamed louder letting him know I was soon going to cum.

"KYLE!"

"CUM FOR ME BABY!" I began to cum para his demand. My liquids gushed out of me, as my body shook. Waves of pure ecstasy took over my body. I felt his hot liquid gushing into my vagina. It was a wonderful feeling.

He fell on top of me. We just laid there, connected at our loins. Our breathing was rapid and our bodies were sweaty. The room smelt of sex and sweat, but was a wonderful smell to me.

After our breathing slowed down, he rolled off of me. "Let's go shower." He got up, letting out a grunt in the process.

I stood up and watched him walk into the bathroom. The muscles in his back were always so hot to me. And his tight butt, don't even get me started. I walked into the bathroom with a smile on my face.

I feel like the happiest girl in the world.

(A/N) forgive me for taking so long, but I am trying to be a good scholar. Also...

We recently got a new schedule because it's a new semester. And this 9th grader who was in my 1st semester class is also in my 2nd semester class and we sit at the same table group. She was like "Where's your boyfriend? Finally the class doesn't have to see you guys flirting all the time." I was so confused who she was talking about. Until I realized she was talking about my crush. And apparently, everyone thought we were dating, crushing on each other, or good exes. But yeah... just wanted to let you know that that happened.

(32) Friendly Intruders

▢▢TRIGGER WARNING!!! THIS CHAPTER CONTAINS ABUSE AND MURDER. PLEASE BE WARY AND READ AT YOUR OWN RISK.

Ashley's POV

Once we exited the shower, we dried each other off, and walked out naked the bathroom. As soon as we walked out, we heard cabinets in the kitchen opening and closing. We also heard a woman and a man speaking.

I looked at Kyle with a scared expression and his expression was one of worry. "Go get dressed while I handle this."

I looked at him as if he were crazy. "You're gonna go fight people in towel? What if your towel falls? Then they're gonna see your dick." He smirked and walked out the room. I went into the closet and quickly moisturized my body. I put on a black bralette with matching underwear. I left my hair in the towel, so that it could be somewhat dry later on.

I tiptoed out of his room and peeked out to the main area. I saw Kyle speaking to a man and a woman, they looked like they were having an engaging conversation. I walked over to Kyle, while watching them carefully. The man was the first to see me and he looked curious. Kyle turned around, his eyes went wide and he tried to shoo me back to his room.

"Kyle, is this another one of those women that you like to play around with?" The man spoke up. The woman next to him slapped the man's shoulder.

I looked at the older couple. I noticed that he woman looked a lot like Kyle. She had blue eyes, and brown hair. She looked to be around 5'9, which seems pretty tall to me. The man however, looked nothing like Kyle. He had dark brown eyes and dark brown hair.

"That's not nice, Henry." The woman said to the man.

"Don't ever say that about her, do you understand." Kyle seemed a little upset, so I grabbed his fist and he seemed to relax a little. He sighed, trying to get control of his temper.

"Mom, Henry. This is my girlfriend Ashley. Ashley, meet my mom and Henry." I wondered why he didn't say mom and dad, but that's a story for another time. I shook their hands and gave them a sweet smile.

"My names Brenda and you can guess my husband's name." She said sweetly. I nodded and went back to Kyle's side.

"You never told me what you were doing here." He said rudely. He wanted them out, probably because he was still somewhat naked.

"You're older sister wanted to tell us all something, I have no idea what it is. We are meeting up at our house on Tuesday next week. At 5:30 pm, you better not be late." Henry said.

"You have an older sister?" I spoke up. Kyle looked down at me. He looked annoyed. But I don't know if I'm the one annoying him or not. I haven't even said anything this whole time. He let go of my hand. Well that answers my question.

"Ok, I'll be there." He started to escort them out the pent, careful to not let his towel drop. I walked into my room and closed the door. I took the towel off my head and threw it against the door. It would prevent him from coming in easily. I heard the front door close right before I put my earbuds in. I played some music and laid in my bed.

I couldn't help but think what I could've done to annoy Kyle.

I heard a banging sound on my door a few minutes after listening to music and texting Chase. I took an earbud out so I could hear better.

"ASHLEY GOD DAMMIT. OPEN THIS FUCKING DOOR!" I hopped out of bed quickly and removed the towel. The door swung open, luckily it didn't hit me. I looked up and saw an angry Kyle.

The way he was staring at me, scares me. I looked down at my toes, trying to ignore his death glare.

"What the fuck were you doing?" He asked angrily.

"Nothing." I said quietly, not wanting to anger him further.

"Then why the fuck didn't you answer the door when I knocked? Why the fuck did you have a towel behind the door?" I shrugged my shoulders. What the frick was his problem?

"Are you mad at me or something?" He asked angrily, but this time a little quieter.

I looked up at him. And he relaxed. He wrapped me in his arms and held me tight.

"I'm so sorry babe. I'm sorry. I shouldn't have yelled." He picked me up and walked over to his bed. He laid me down and started kissing me deeply and lovingly. I kissed him back. I love him, I love him so much but sometimes he gets on my nerves.

I stopped kissing me and he got off. "Tell me what's wrong."

"Why don't we ever talk about your life? Why don't we ever talk about mine? Why is it that we barely know each other and we have sex all the time?"

Kyle sighed and slid his palm over his face. "Do you wanna talk about my family or yours?"

"Tell me about your family. Let me get to know you better."

•••

Kyle's POV

She wants to get to know me better? There's a reason I don't talk about my past with people. But I guess I should let her in.

"Okay then. Let's start." I got in her bed and sat next to her. "I was born in Summerlin, Nevada on August 18th. I had a sister, Bianca, who was 3 years older than me and two parents whom I thought loved each other. As I grew up, my sister and I were close. She stuck up for me, even though we fought like regular siblings. When I was younger, I really didn't know that all the fighting in between my parents was abnormal. When I was around 8, I saw my dad come home drunk. He was upset. He saw my mom and started yelling at her. My sister ran into the living room where everyone was at. My dad punched her in her jaw and spit on her. My sister got the house phone and called the police on him. Sadly, my mom didn't want to press charges, because she loved my dad or maybe she was scared. A few days later he came back and apologized. My sister and I started being more careful around our father and his outrageous temper. Months passed, they still fought, but he was never physical. During the summer, I came home and saw my mom laying on the floor and broken glass around her. She was badly beaten and unconscious. I called 911 and they came. I called my sister on the house phone and she came back from a friend's house."

I felt the tears welling up in my eyes. I really don't want to cry in front of Ashley. I'm supposed to be strong. Not a crybaby.

"Babe, you don't have to finish right now. It's fine." She hugged me and started kissing my face. I shook my head.

I took a deep breath and continued. "At the hospital, they fixed her up and the police came in. They needed to know what happened. Me being young and not knowing any better, I told them it was my dad. That probably gave my mom the courage to speak up. Shortly after, they found my dad and arrested him. My mom didn't want to sue, so she just settled with him going to jail. He got 7 years, which definitely wasn't long enough. We moved to a smaller house and life started over."

"When I was about 15, life for my mom got harder. She was living paycheck to paycheck and sometimes she didn't have enough money for basic stuff. My sister went to college and my mom tried to help with that. I wanted to help her out, it was hard seeing my mom struggle. I knew Chase and he sold drugs. He made a few hundred weekly, so I asked him how to start. He helped me out. I started selling whatever drug I could get my hands on. Weed, coke, meth, Xanax, and codeine. I started making around $500-$800 a week. A lot of people came to me for their drugs. I started putting around $300 in my mom's wallet and then $400. At first she never asked any questions. But after a while she got curious. I told her I got a job by helping people with homework."

"You'd be surprised, your boyfriend was a straight A student." I chuckled and Ashley smiled.

"So she just nodded. She would deposit the cash and soon enough, we weren't living paycheck to paycheck. After about a year, Chase and I got closer. He was like the brother I never had. We hung out all the time, sold drugs and did homework together. Life was a lot better. By the time I graduated high school, I was the Valedictorian and still had straight A's. I was a really popular kid. I had sex with a lot of people and couldn't keep a serious relationship. I didn't play any sports or anything. I had gotten a full ride to UCLA, so I went. I majored in business. I studied until I got a Masters degree in business. Oh, when I was 19, that's when I started my own gang. I wanted to make money while going to school. I bought my first car and it was great. At first it was just Chase and I, but we expanded. We then got Wesley and Jacob, then Victor. When I was 22, my mom remarried to Henry. He made her happy, so I was happy for her."

"Sounds nice." Ashley said quietly. I looked at her and she was looking out the window. I couldn't help myself from admiring her. She's beautiful.

"This is where I.... this is where it gets bad. Do you still wanna hear it?" She nodded and gave my hand a reassuring squeeze.

"So a few weeks after the wedding and my mom and Henry had gotten back from their honeymoon, my dad showed up. Not to see me, but to try to hurt my mom. Luckily, I had been on my way there to fix the toilet. I pull up to the house and hear yelling, and you know what I do for a living. So I always have my gun on me. I ran into the house with my gun out. I saw my dad, Henry and my mom yelling at each other. My dad had a broken liquor bottle and Henry was trying to defend my mom. Without a second thought, I fired. I shot and killed my dad. I didn't shoot him once. After the first shot, I shot him 4 more times. My mom and Henry were scared. I dropped my gun and my mom ran up to me and hugged me."

I felt the tears running down my face. Then I felt Ashley's soft fingers doing their best to swipe them away.

"That was the first person I've ever killed. Also, the only person that I cried about after killing them." Ashley sighed. I looked up at her and saw tears welling up in her eyes. I pulled her onto my lap and I let my tears stream freely. I've never showed my emotions this much to any woman.

We sat like that for a while until I gained some composure. I moved some of the hair from her face and kissed her softly. And she returned the favor.

In this moment, I realized how much I needed Ashley. How much I loved her. And especially, how much I wanted her to be in my future.

_____(A/N) Okay, so it's been a while since I updated this book and the truth is that I've been busy. I know I keep saying that, but it's the truth. I started playing softball on my school team. I made VARSITY!!!! I also have my major AP exam coming up. So between school, softball and planning my party, I haven't had much time. But I'm going to try to publish a few chapters during spring break.

Hope you enjoyed this chapter!!!Read, comment, share and vote. DON'T FORGET TO KEEP READING!

Ciao for now

(33) SUPRISE?!

Kyle's POV

I woke up to a pleasurable feeling. Someone was sucking my dïck like a pro. I pushed the sheets down and could see my princess bobbing her head on me. I groaned and she looked up at me with a smile.

"Good morning, Daddy." She winked and went back to blowing me. My hand found its way to the back of her head and pushed her down further on my cöck. She swirled her tongue around the tip of my cöck which made me get closer to cumming. Her head bobbed back up and she spit on the head. With one hand, she stroked my shaft and sucked on the head of my dïck. With the other hand, she fondled my balls and the tension was building up quickly. I needed to release.

"Oh shit, I'm cumming."

She kept her mouth on my dick with her lips sealed tightly around the shaft. I came in her mouth, jet after jet of cum jolting out of my cöck. Ashley opened her mouth and showed me my load, she closed her mouth and swallowed. She smiled like an adorable little girl. Damn, I love this girl. She crawled back up to me, and I kissed her on the forehead.

"Why thank you beautiful! Let me get a taste of you." Ashley got the hint luckily and slid her body until she was sitting on my face. I started eating her out and she squealed. I spelt 'will you marry me' with my tongue for fun. She got a lot of pleasure out of it. She started grinding her pussy over my face and her juices were all over me. I wrapped my arms around her thighs and pulled her closer to my face so that my tongue could enter her. I moved my hand in order to get some of her wetness onto my thumb. Once my thumb was lathered up, I traced her asshole. I slowly pushed my thumb into her ass, I was met with a little resistance, but that wasn't going to stop me. I started thrusting my thumb in and out of her ass slowly. She started moaning louder and calling my name, which was so fucking sexy. I started to flick my tongue on her clit, and that's what pushed her over the edge. She started cumming and screaming. She squirted a little and I swallowed it. I had to push her off my face so that I could breath. After her orgasm subdued, she just laid there.

"Let's go get cleaned up." I said. I grabbed her hand and we walked into the bathroom.

****

"We need to go to the mall later." I stated as we put our dishes in the sink.

"For?"

"We're going to my mom's house tonight, remember?" Ashley nodded. I watched her expressions closely. She didn't seem nervous or frightened about going to meet my family. I on the other hand am. I don't know how I'm going to explain to them how I met Ashley and what our first date was like. When they or if they plan to as me if I want to marry her, should I be honest? I mean, yeah, I want to marry Ashley Isabelle Rowens. But, saying that to someone, is like I'm selling my soul away.

"Uhh Kyle..... Kyle. KYLE!" Ashley snapped me out of my thoughts. She looked at me worriedly, then licked her lips. I love when she does that. I grabbed her waist and pulled her towards me. I planted my lips against hers and kissed her deeply. She kissed me back. Our tongues doing a little dance between our mouths. I grabbed her ass and she scoffed. She took her mouth off of mine and slapped my chest.

"Ow, what was that for?" I said sarcastically with a smile on my face.

"Let's get dressed now, so that we'll have time to shop around and get ready afterwards." I sighed and she chuckled while shaking her head. She grabbed my wrist and pulled me into the bedroom. Sadly, we weren't going to have sex, although later, we can.

While we were in the closet together she started picking an outfit for me. She grabbed some grey, sweat pant material shorts, a black semi-fitted top and some black shoes. I gotta admit, that's a pretty chill outfit. "Let's go pick you an outfit now." I grabbed her hand and led her into her bedroom. I went into her closet and picked out a grey, spaghetti strap, body-con dress and some black Toms. "No bra, no underwear." I said before walking back to my room to get dressed.

"THAT MEANS YOU CAN'T WEAR UNDERWEAR EITHER!!" I heard Ashley yell out. I laughed, that sounds like a deal.

A few minutes later, I walked out of my room ready to go. Ashley was standing at the counter using her iPod. I ran up behind her and smacked her ass. "Damn, baby girl got cake." I smiled.

"Ouch. Are you ready to go?" She smiled and nodded.

"First let me do an panty check." I got down one knee and raised her leg. I lifted up the tight dress and saw the lips of her pussy, and her little clit sticking out. I gave it a quick kiss and stood back up. She fixed her dress, then I fondled her boobs. She wasn't wearing a bra, I knew that because I saw her nipples poking out, but I really wanted to touch her boobs. "Ok, all clear. Let's go."

I started walking towards the door because I already had everything I needed. I heard Ashley clear her throat. I turned around and raised an eyebrow. "What?"

She smiled and strutted toward me. "I need to check you, of course." I clenched my jaw. Dirty thoughts started filling my head and it's taking a lot to not act upon them. She slid her hand down the front of my shorts. She took a hold of my dick and started stroking it. She looked into my eyes with a pure look of seduction. She doesn't understand how hard I am and how hard it is to control myself right now. I let out a groan and she quickly took her hand out of my shorts.

"All clear." She winked and headed for the door. I grabbed her wrist and pulled her towards me. I kissed her, a forceful and lustful kiss. "C'mon Daddy, we can't be late!" She said playfully and winked at me. I walked out the door and we started out to my car.

****

"C'mon Beautiful, let me see how it looks." I said frustrated. We had been at the mall for at least 3 hours and we still haven't found a dress for her to wear. She walked out of the fitting room looking like a complete angel. I was in complete and utter awe. She was wearing a short skater dress that had light pink flowers around the bodice, which faded to an all white dress starting at the waist down. She came out smiling and I knew that this was the one. This was the dress she wanted.

"I want this one." She said happily and clasped her hands in front of her body. I stood up from the bench I was seated on and wrapped my arms around her waist. I pulled her small body towards me and kissed her forcefully and lustfully. I picked her up and walked into the fitting room and closed the door behind us. I put her down so that I could unzip the back of her dress. As I did that, she started lifting my shirt off of my body. Once my shirt was off and I had finished unzipping her dress, her dress fell to the floor and I saw her more than perfect body. Her nipples standing alert and the perky breasts on which they stood. Her small waist that I loved snaking my arms around, just to pull her closer to me. Her mound, her beautiful shaved mound that tasted like honey and just the perfect amount of tart. My eyes went down her luscious tanned legs that wrap love to wrap around me while I'm buried inside of her. My eyes shot back up to that lovely face of hers. The one that caught my attention not too long ago. Her plump, pink lips that I love to kiss, suck and bite on.

I can't fuck her, I need to make love to her. I need to make love to this woman that I love dearly. I bit my lip and she sunk down onto her knees. "No baby doll. We'll have to come back to this later. Right now, we need to get our clothes back on, continue shopping and then go home." I grabbed my shirt off the floor and put it back on. When Ashley picked up the dress, it was somewhat wrinkled, so we'll just have to get another one that no one has tried on. Once she was dressed, we walked out the fitting room and there was a sales associate looking at me. "Excuse me, can you get me another one of these dresses in a 6 please." I said with a smile. The sales associate blushed and went to do what I asked.

"I need shoes, jewelry and uhhh...." I raised my eyebrow. Ashley was thinking about what else she might need before going to my Mom's house. "Ice cream!" She said, breaking the silence.

"Here you go Sir." The sales associate said to me as she handed me the dress. I nodded and she walked away. Ashley and I walked to the check-out and luckily there wasn't a long line.

"I don't think you need ice cream, I think you need to rest when we get home." She shook her head.

"No. I'm pretty sure I need ice cream, because I'm not tired." She yawned and it was sexy. Every little thing about her is sexy. "Well, even if I was tired, which I'm not. I wouldn't have time to sleep because we have to go home, take a shower and then get on the road."

"You can sleep in the car on the way to my Mom's house." I said as I handed the man at the register the dress. I peered at the register.

"That'll be 289 dollars and 72 cents." I handed him my debit card and he quickly swiped it.

"Ugh. Why can't I just have ice cream? You're being so difficult." She pouted.

"One, because it's going to spoil your appetite. Two, because you'll be hyper. And three, because..."

"Here's your dress and your debit card. Have a wonderful afternoon!" I grabbed the dress, which was in a large bag the covered the whole thing.

I handed Ashley the dress to hold while we continued to look for some shoes and jewelry for her.

"Just letting you know, you only gave me two reasons why I can't have ice cream. And for me to actually accept your answer, there need to be 3 reasons. Sooo... That means I can get ice cream. Let's go to Haagen-Dazs!"

"How about this? You can get ice cream, as long as you pay for it." I said and she smiled and then scowled at me.

"That's totally not fair. When you had me.." She looked around and whispered "ya know." Then she started speaking to me in her regular voice. "It's not like you had whatever his name is, grab my wallet."

"Well if Victor had grabbed your wallet. Then you would've had your debit card. Then whenever you made transactions, the police and your family could've tracked you. Then I wouldn't be your amazing boyfriend because I would be in jail." She rolled her eyes at me. We walked into a shoe store and I saw a pair of heels that matched her skin tone. I walked straight to them and picked them up. They were Louis Vuitton, perfect. "What size heel do you wear, baby cakes?"

"7 and a half." I flagged the closest person down and asked them to get me the heels in a 7 and a half.

****

I looked at the clock in the car as I drove to my Mom's house. Ashley had went to sleep as soon as I started driving. It was approximately 5:10, luckily we were only had about 4 minutes left until we reach my Mom's. As soon as I pulled up on the driveway, I saw my Mom and her husband's car, my sister's and that's it. I guess we're the last ones to arrive. I turned off the car and got out. I went to the passenger door, opened it and kissed Ashley on her lips. She woke up softly and fluttered her eyes.

"Are we here?" She asked softly. I nodded and she unbuckled her seat belt. I helped her out the car and we walked up to the front door. I rung the doorbell and the door opened a few seconds afterwards.

"Hey honey." My mom said happily as she opened her arms to hug me. I gave her a hug and she greeted Ashley as well. We walked inside and Ashley's eyes wandered. I heard shriek, it sounded like an animal being killed. I looked to see what could've made that god forbidden sound and it was my awesome big sister.

"HEY LITTLE BROTHER!!! I BET YOU MISSED ME. DIDN'T YA?" Bianca said excitedly. She gave me a tight hug and wouldn't let go. She shook me as she held onto me. I tried to hug her back, but her arms were wrapped tightly around me. She inhaled a lot of air and let go of me. "And who might this female that came home with my little brother be?" She asked as she stared at Ashley. I could tell Ashley was a little weirded out by my sister, so I decided to introduce them.

"Um. Bianca this is my girlfriend Ashley. Ashley, this is my annoying older sister, Bianca." As soon as I said annoying, Bianca swatted my arm. She's always hitting me. She's lucky I won't hit her back right now. Bianca hugged Ashley and Ashley returned the favor. It was a quick hug. After Bianca released Ashley, I grabbed my baby girl's hand.

"I can't believe an actual girl actually has an interest in my little brother. Like who would've thought that a pretty girl would like Kyle? Cause I definitely didn't."

"Alright, c'mon kids. Dinner is ready." We all walked into the dinning room and sat down. I pulled out the chair for Ashley because I'm such a gentleman. I sat down next to her and we all said grace.

We started eating our dinner, there was steak, baked potatoes, grilled asparagus, and cream of corn. My sister stood up abruptly, looking like a nervous animal who was unsure of humans.

"Okay, so I have to tell you guys something and I hope you guys don't hate me after I tell you this. Promise me you won't hate me." I was confused as to why she thinks that anyone could hate her, she's such an awesome person. "Okay, so you all know Karen. Except for you Ashley. Well anyway..." Bianca took a deep breath and closed her eyes. "Karen and I aren't just friends. We're together, as in girlfriend and girlfriend. As in I'm a lesbian." I was beyond shocked. I mean, when we were younger, she didn't have many boyfriend's, but that was understandable. Guys were douche bags. But she likes girls.

"Awe. I'm glad you're coming out. And you guys are a very cute couple. I would say you guys are as cute as Kyle and I but look at us, we're unbeatable." I heard Ashley say. Everyone looked at her. Karen and Bianca were smiling, probably happy that Ashley was making light of the situation. I looked back at Bianca and she mouthed 'thank you' to Ashley.

"Well honey. I'm glad that you found out who you are as a person and who you are attracted to. But, I just need to say this. Don't ever make me promise not to hate you, because I made that promise when you were born and I'm never going to break that promise." Bianca started tearing up, so my Mom stood up and went to give Bianca a hug. I looked over to Henry and saw a face of confusion. He can ask questions later, but for now, we have to accept my sister as she is. I mean, I had to accept her as a mean, ugly little troll for my whole life who was also related to me, so her being a lesbian won't bother me.

"When are you going to come out as a troll because I've been waiting to hear that since I was like 7?" I asked sarcastically. Ashley nudged my arm.

"Bianca is sexy, not a troll doofus. That's why you have a hard time finding girl friends." Karen said, finally breaking her silence.

"For your information, I'm never going to have to find a girlfriend ever again. And many girls want a ride on my -"

"OKAY! So who wants dessert?" My mom interrupted me before I could finish what I was going to say.

"Dessert sounds great Sweetie!" Henry said. Everyone started clearing the table and bringing their dishes to the kitchen sink. Once everyone got a slice of pie, they went to the living room to watch a movie, while Ashley and I stayed in the kitchen.

"You're so fucking beautiful. Do you know that?" I asked Ashley before lifting her onto the counter. She giggled as I nuzzled her neck.

"You're very handsome yourself." She said. I could feel her smile and I had a feeling she was blushing. I started kissing and sucking her neck and she let out quiet moans. My hand slid in between her legs and found the sweet spot that rested in the center of her being. I started to massage her clit to make her wet, but I didn't have to do much, because she was already aroused. I pulled my fingers away and tasted them. Sweet like honey with a hint of tartness. I brought my fingers back down and started to slowly finger her. She let out quiet whimpers and moans and her head fell back. I started kissing her neck more.

"Ew. Get a room you horny little kids." I heard my sister Bianca say.

"Technically a kitchen is a room and you're invading our space."

"I don't think so. This is a public area, how do you think Mom would feel about your girlfriend's juices being on the counter?" Ashley pulled my hand out from in between her legs. Redness crept its way onto her soft cheeks.

"And you wonder why it took you your whole life to find someone that actually likes you."

"Actually, Karen and I started dating 2 years ago. I just wasn't ready to come out." I turned around and looked at her amazed.

"Wow, how could you keep such a big secret from your little brother? I feel hurt."

"It's too bad that I don't care." She shrugged and left the kitchen. I sighed. That's my sister and I's relationship in a nut shell. It has its ups and downs.

"Wanna continue this upstairs?" I winked and smiled to Ashley.

"Nope. We are going to eat this sweet potato pie and spend time with your family." I groaned and she hopped off the counter.

She might not want to have sex right now, but that won't keep me from loving her forever.

(A/N) I feel really bad for not consistently updating this book and I'm really sorry. I had to leave my dad's house because of some drama and basically he doesn't want me anymore so yeah. But anyway.... IM OBSESSED WITH KYLE. YA KNOW SUPERDUPERKYLE?!?!? Ughh. I wanna see him in concert. And my friends who are a part of the LGBTQ+ community basically told me I was an ally today and I didn't know what that meant so they told me and I was like, that's lit.

I hope y'all liked this chapter and don't forget to vote, comment, share and keep reading.

I'm out.

(34) A New Plan

Ashley's POV

I looked at the clock hanging on the wall and it was already 11:25 pm. We were all getting off the couch ready to go to bed. Kyle and I hadn't planned to stay here overnight, so we didn't have a change of clothes or any of our toiletries. I stood up and stretched, while doing so, a yawn escaped my mouth. Kyle looked at me and smirked.

"Awe, someone's tired." He mocked me so I slapped his arm.

"Am not. When people yawn, they don't necessarily need to be tired. Sometimes they yawn when their brain needs more oxygen. And it so happens that my brain needed more oxygen. Thank you very much." I had to hit him with the facts, or else he will always make fun of me for not being able to stay up late.

"Wow, thanks for the info. Einstein. Now, how about you march your pretty little sleepy ass up those stairs." I rolled my eyes and started walking towards the stairs that I saw earlier.

While climbing up the stairs, I stopped and looked at Kyle following behind me. "By the way, my butt isn't little. And you know it." I said with a devilish smirk. I saw him bite his lip and his eyes averted to my butt. I started walking up the stairs more sexually, knowing that I was making him hard under his pants.

"Keep it up and we might be staying up tonight. And so will everybody else." I walked to the top of the stairs and he was right behind me.

"Okay, so where's your room?" He moved to in front of me and led me to his room. It was navy blue with dark wooden furniture. I sat on the bed and looked around. His room wasn't huge, but it definitely wasn't small either. I was surprised to see everything clean, no dust, a clean carpet and fresh sheets. I saw some books and journals on his desk. I got up from the bed and grabbed a journal. I started flipping through the pages and skimming over them. I skimmed over an interesting page and decided to actually read it.

'Today was fucking bad. Last week the school told all the 7th grade students to bring their fathers to the school for an early father's day breakfast. But, I don't have a father. Well not a good one anyway. I still remember that bastard. He was a horrible drunk who abused his wife. My mom. How could anyone hurt her? I fucking hate him. He should rot in jail. Well anyways, the breakfast only reminded me of what an asshole of a father I had, if I could even call him a father. He was more like a person that paid the bills once in a while and bought food. But, there was a good thing that happened today. Katelyn Vargas gave me her number. She's soooo hot. All the guys in my middle school like her. She's got big boobs, a big butt and she's funny. I wouldn't mind her being my girlfriend.'

I looked up at Kyle to see him still rummaging through his dresser and closet, searching for clothes that I could wear. I put the journal down and went to hug him. I wrapped my arms around his body as he faced the other direction. "Baby girl, are you okay?"

"I love you." I said those words. The words that can make your heart feel likes it's racing a fighter jet or make it melt like chocolate. I turned around and kissed her forehead.

"I love you more." I backed up and crossed my arms? I was disappointed. In our time of romance, he just has to be a step higher than me. Ugh.

"There you go again. Always one-upping me. I tell you that I love you and you have to love me more. Don't ya?" She rolled her eyes and crossed her arms.

"I cant be one-upping you if it's true." He winked at me and smiled.

I put my hands on my hips and repeated what he said, but I made it sound stupider. "I cAn'T bE OnE-UpPiNg yOu iF ItS TrUe."

He chuckled, but I honestly didn't think it was funny. "Here you ugly little duck. It's a shirt."

I grabbed it from him and held it out in front of me to see how big it was. It wasn't too big, unlike his shirts now. I started stripping right there in front of him and his eyes were glued to my body. I slid the shirt over my head and he snapped out of it. I crawled into bed and watched him get dressed. He got in bed next to me and turned the lamps off. We spooned; with his arms holding me and the warmth of his body surrounding me, I quickly fell asleep.

••*•*•*•*•*•*•*•*•*•*•*•*•*•*•*•*•*•*

Kyle's POV

I woke up and checked my phone. Shit. Only 15%, I left my charger in the car because I hadn't thought that Ashley and I would be spending the night. It was 7:00, I just stared at her. At Ashley, the woman I loved. And hopefully, I'll be able to love her forever. I stared at her cute little face and the lips that I love sucking on and kissing. Her beautiful brown hair that surrounded her as if it were her halo. I wanna marry her. I want to marry Ashley Isabelle Rowens. I want to have kids with her, have a big house and be happy with her forever. I grabbed my phone, sadly it only had 15% left. I looked up proposal ideas on the internet. I wanted this proposal to go well. I wanted her to be happy and so in the moment that she'll say yes. I found a website with 50 great proposal ideas, so I clicked on the link. I quickly scrolled through it. Restaurant, a dance number, singing, signs, a shirt, a dog, vacation, sex, an airplane banner, and etc.

The restaurant idea lingered in my head, so I knew I had to do it. Ashley loves food anyway, so she'll be satisfying her hunger at the restaurant, then I'll be satisfying her desires afterwards.

I got up and went to the hallway bathroom to brush my teeth. Luckily, my mom had spare toothbrushes and deodorant. I used it and went downstairs for a glass of water. My sister and her girlfriend were making out. She had Karen on the counter and she was in between her legs. I could clearly see that my sister's fingers were in between Karen's legs and also, Karen isn't the quietest person in the world. But the sight almost made me vomit.

"Eww. Get a room." I said disgusted. No doubt my face was twisted with a look of disgust. My sister turned around quickly, probably spooked that I had caught her in the same position I had Ashley in last night.

"What the actual fuck? You could've made your presence clear." Bianca said while wiping her fingers off on her shorts.

"Ew no. Why would I want to be a part of your fingering session with your girlfriend. Ya see, if I had made myself known, you would've taken your time to clean up. But if I scare you, then you'll hurry up and end the session." I explained while getting a bottle of water out of the fridge.

"Whatever. Can you go somewhere else, I was kinda busy here."

"No, I'm getting a glass of water. And how do you think Mom would feel if she knew Karen's juices were all over the counter?" I said mocking her. Karen blushed and crossed her legs, while Bianca looked angry.

"You wouldn't dare." She seethed.

"You're. I rather not have to describe how you were fingering Karen. Ew, it sounds nasty just summarizing it." I cringed.

"Oh grow up. Did you need something or are you just going to keep standing here?" Bianca was quickly growing annoyed with my presence, I can tell not much has changed since we were younger.

I took a deep breath in and said it aloud for the first time ever. "I want to marry Ashley." Bianca's eyes went wide and she jumped up and ran toward me. She engulfed me with her long arms and shook me.

"HOLY SMOKE! YOU WANT TO GET MARRIED?!" She said loudly. I broke out of her grip before she could say it again and I covered her mouth.

"Shut up before anyone else hears you." I removed my hand and her mouth was still wide open with a smile. I looked over to Karen who was also smiling. "I need help picking out a ring and stuff. I already know how I'm going to propose and I can't tell you because it's a surprise."

"Did you tell Mom?" I shook my head. "Well go tell her, we can go ring shopping today. Do you know what ring size Ashley wears?"

"No, because she doesn't wear rings." While I was saying that, Bianca was already on her way up the stairs. Karen hopped off the counter.

"Congrats Kyle. You're finally going to stick with one girl." Karen teased. I rolled my eyes. I went back to my room to check on Ashley and she was still asleep. Someone knocked on the bed room door so I went and opened it, it was my mom. She pulled me into the hallway and had a huge grim on her face.

"Is it true Kyle? Please tell me it's true!" I nodded and I couldn't help but smile. She engulfed me in a tight hug and rocked side to side. "Oh my God. You're getting married. I'm so proud of you and I'm happy that you're happy." She let go of me and looked at me. "We need to get a ring."

"I know. Bianca was asking me about Ashley's ring size, but how the hell am I supposed to know it. It's not something you just talk about in a conversation."

"When she wakes up, ask her to try my ring on. If she fits it then I'll know what size to get. If its too tight then we'll get a bigger size and if it's too big, then we'll get a bigger size." I nodded. How am I supposed to ask her to try a ring on without her suspecting anything. The door opened and there stood a sleepy looking Ashley.

"Good morning. What's happening out here?" I looked at my mom and gulped.

"On nothing sweetie. Do you own any rings, I'm about to clean mine and I was wondering if I could clean yours as well?" Ashley tried to think. I knew she was tired, so her brain wasn't fully awake yet.

"Yeah, but it's at my house. My friend gave it to me before he moved away." I was shocked. A guy that I've never heard about gave my girlfriend a ring?

"Oh that's sweet. You see Kyle, you should've been a gentleman like Ashley's friend. Instead doing the nonsense that you were doing. What size was it, do you know?" My Mom crossed her arms in a playful way and I rolled my eyes.

"Pretty sure it was a six." Ashley answered tiredly.

"That nonsense is the reason that I have a successful restaurant and a nice penthouse." I smiled, proud of my accomplishments.

"Whatever hun. Why don't you go join Ashley and we can go to a few jewelers later?" I looked beside me and saw that Ashley had left me. I went into the room and saw her sleeping peacefully in my bed. I'm excited to marry her. She's so fucking sexy.

I got into the bed with her and pulled her towards my body.

****

"Mom, I need to make a quick call. Can you just keep looking at rings and pick the best one?"

"Hey Chase. What you up to?"

Oh nothing. What's up?

"I'm ring shopping for Ashley. I need your help with something."

Hold up. Ring shopping? For what?

"To get married idiot. I'm going to propose in 3 days. But I need your help with something."

Dude, don't you think you're moving a little fast?

"Nah. Can you help me?" I was starting to grow impatient.

With?

"The proposal man. I'm taking her to Yum, and some other things. I just need you to have the restaurant ready."

What do you mean ready?

"A table just for her and I. Flowers that are white and possibly gold. I'm going to send you a list of songs that are romantic, and you have to choose one so that it can play while I'm proposing to her."

Damn, anything else?

"Dude, just fucking do it. I want the best table in the restaurant where everyone can see us. Alright? Bye." With that, I hung up. I had so much more in plan for Ashley, she was going to be so surprised.

****

I was looking at the ring my mom chose for Ashley, it was beautiful. It was shaped as a crown with diamonds decorating it. It was perfect, Ashley is my princess and she deserves to wear a crown. I bought the ring and asked for a red box with a white bow, and that's exactly what they gave me. I walked out the store and for the first time in a while, I was content, excited and nervous at the same time. My mom and I went to a dress shop and got Ashley a strapless navy blue pouf dress. I didn't have to worry about shoes or jewelry because Ashley has those items.

"Are you excited Kyle?"

I nodded, "And quite nervous. What if she says no?" I asked my mom. My mom chuckled as if it were funny. "I'm serious, what if she says no? I'll look like a fool in front of everybody." I told her.

"Kyle honey. She's not going to say no. The way she looks at you when you're looking at her, even when you're not— she adores you. If she says no, it's probably because she's not ready. But I doubt that Ashley is going to say no when you propose."

We walked to the car and drove back to her house. Now I gotta figure out where to hide this box and how am I supposed to act as if everything is normal when it isn't?

••*•*•*•*•*•*•*•*•*•*•*•*•*•*•*•*•*

Chase's POV

I was currently at the restaurant making sure everything was perfect, just as Kyle asked me to do. To be honest, I still have feelings for Ashley. What can I say, she's gorgeous, smart, funny, sexy and a few other things. And for him to ask me to help him propose was like the ultimate test. I am quite angry he couldn't have asked Sam or someone else to do it, but I guess since I'm the Co-Founder of Yum, it would have to be me.

I placed an order for the best champagne in the country to arrive here in 2 days. I'm getting new table clothes and candles. I also found some roses that were white, and the florist is willing to put gold flakes on them. Everyone at the restaurant was working hard to make Kyle's dream come true. God damn, I sound like a fucking wedding planner.

"Sir, everything is ready. We'll keep everything in tip-top shape until his proposal. We can decorate then." I nodded and walked it of the restaurant. The fresh air really helped clear my mind. I got in the car and drove off to my house. Cristina was there waiting for me to get back. I mean, if Kyle doesn't want her, then I'll take her. She's not Grade A like Ashley, but she'll do.

(A/N) Guys only a 1 or 2 more chapters left. Get ready to be shooketh and flabbergasted. After this story is finished, I'll start working on a werewolf story, in which I am very excited about!

I can't believe that Kyle is finally settling down. I also can't believe that Chase is fucking Cristina because he's in his feelings. He must be into having Kyle's sloppy seconds.

Keep on reading, commenting, voting and sharing. Adios my woes .

(35) Here it Goes

Kyle's POV

I made a few calls 3 days ago. I needed some people to watch as I proposed to Ashley. And today's the day. They all said that they would be at the restaurant at 6:30. Then, I'll propose at 7:15.

****

"C'MON ASHLEY!" I yelled from the living room. She was taking too long to get dressed. It was already 6:40. The restaurant called and asked if I were on my way and I said yes. But I'm not because Ashley is taking too long. I checked my inner jacket pocket to make sure I still had her ring. And I did. I put the box back in my pocket and as soon as I did that she walked out. She's gorgeous.

"Fuck." I looked her up and down and she did a little twirl for me. "You look... beautiful as fuck, baby girl." I grabbed her and kissed her lips. I grabbed her hand and led her out the pent house. We had to walk quickly."

"Kyle, why are we in such a hurry?"

I ignored her question. But then I realized that she might get mad at me and I didn't want her angry at me tonight.

"I made a reservation at my restaurant and it's important that we are there in time. Something big is happening tonight."

Once we were in the car, I quickly left the parking garage and sped on the streets. Careful not to cause my car accidents, because seeing people die for no reason when I'm the cause of it is horrible. We arrived at the restaurant at 6:50 and we were seated immediately. I ordered our champagne and food. The table was set up perfectly. We started eating as soon as the food came out the kitchen. Luckily it was still warm. I looked at my watch and it was 7:15. I stood up and Ashley's eyes shot up to me and I could sense she was confused.

I took a big breath and exhaled. "I haven't known you for 3 years, not even one. My eyes first laid upon your sexiness while you were out with your friends. I brought you into my life and we soon became friends. Then I realized I was in love with you. Deeply, in love with you. The way your face scrunches up when you don't like something, or when your beautiful long legs carry you to the refrigerator. The way your voice sounds early in the morning to how your voice sounds when you're excited." I looked around the restaurant and people were staring at me, at us. "Ashley, I want to spend the rest of my life with you." I got down on one knee while reaching into my pocket to grab the ring box. I pulled it out and Ashley stood up. I could see the tears welling up in the eyes that I get lost in. I said these following words loudly, they were important for me and everyone else. "Ashley Isabelle Rowens, will you do me the honor of marrying me?" I was nervous. She smiled and started nodding. The tears were rolling down her cheeks as I slipped the ring onto her finger. I stood up and kissed her passionately and everyone was clapping and saying 'aw'.

"ASHLEY?!" I heard a man say. I looked at where the voice came from and saw her father. I was happy that he didn't think the phone call to him and his family was a prank. But, I was nervous about meeting him. Then I heard a female say Ashley the same way, it came from where Dylan was sitting, that girl must be Taylor. Ashley's family and her best friend came running to the table and Ashley looked shocked.

They engulfed her in a hug, tears rolling down their faces.

"Ashley, we've missed you."

---

www.ingramcontent.com/pod-product-compliance
Lightning Source LLC
Chambersburg PA
CBHW071955070526
44583CB00015B/1198